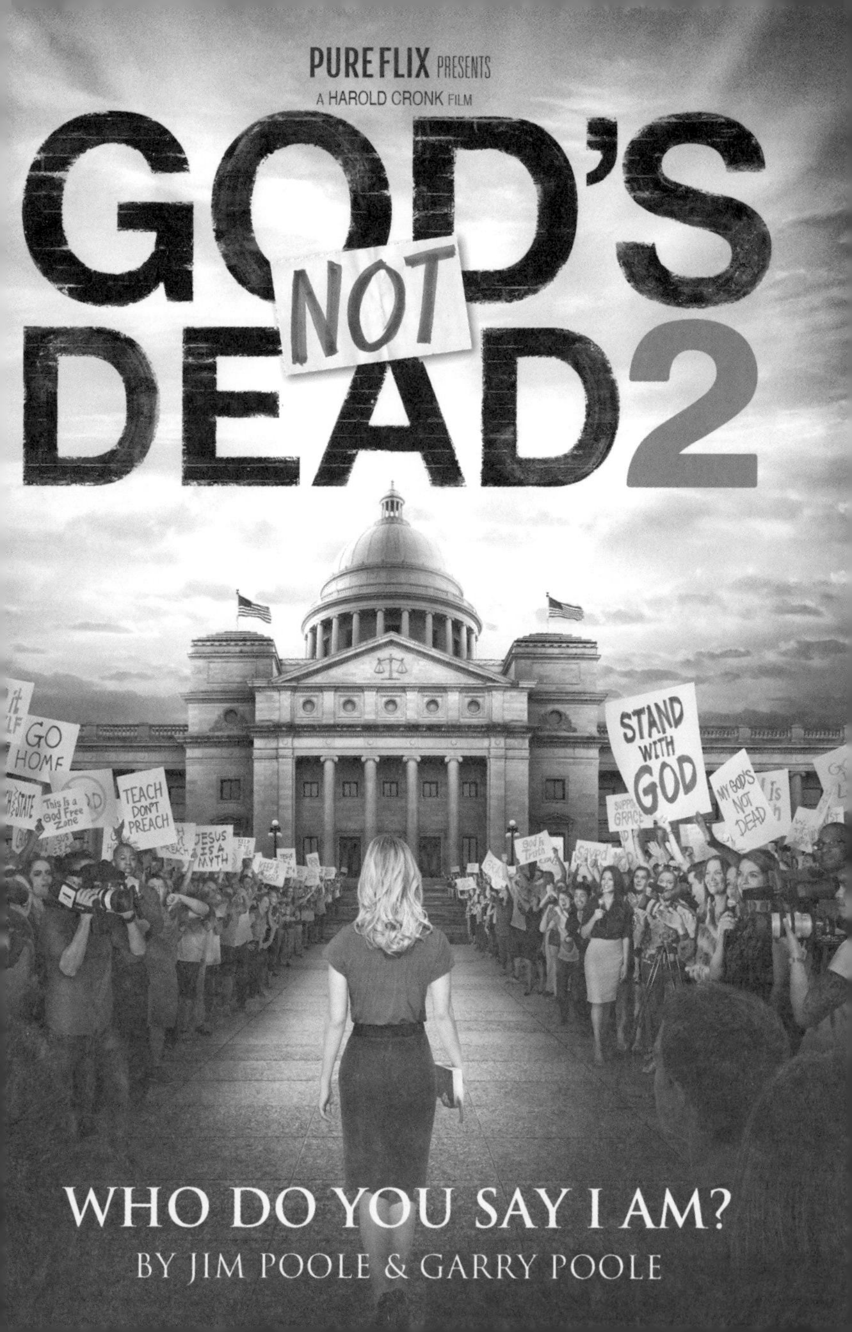
PURE FLIX PRESENTS
A HAROLD CRONK FILM
GOD'S NOT DEAD 2
GO HOME
This Is a God Free Zone
TEACH DON'T PREACH
JESUS IS A MYTH
STAND WITH GOD
MY GOD'S NOT DEAD
WHO DO YOU SAY I AM?
BY JIM POOLE & GARRY POOLE

OUTREACH®

God's Not Dead 2: Who Do You Say I Am?

Published by Outreach, Inc., Colorado Springs, CO 80919
www.Outreach.com

ISBN: 9781942027911
Cover Design by Tim Downs
Interior Design by Alexia Garaventa
Written by Jim Poole and Garry Poole

Printed in the United States of America

CONTENTS

GO
N
DE

Because here's something else that's weird but true: in the day-to-day trenches of adult life, there is actually no such thing as atheism. There is no such thing as not worshipping. Everybody worships. The only choice we get is what to worship.
—*David Foster Wallace*

You're gonna have to serve somebody.
—*Bob Dylan*

Suppose you expressed a belief you firmly held—a deep, personal conviction that shapes the very core of who you are—and the act of merely talking about it was declared illegal. How would you feel? How would you react? What would you do?

At the heart of the movie *God's Not Dead 2*, Grace Wesley, a history teacher who is a devoted Christian, answers a student's question about Jesus. She is careful with her answer, yet confident about quoting a Bible verse. She'd been teaching about Martin Luther King Jr., so it was quite natural for her to respond to the student's inquiry comparing Jesus's ideals with those of the civil rights leader and former minister. However, when parents and school administrators find out about the incident, Grace is accused of crossing the line of what's acceptable—by "preaching and proselytizing her personal faith" in the classroom.

As the case goes to court, the prosecuting attorney builds a strong case against Grace for inappropriately overstepping the wall of separation between church and state as articulated by Thomas Jefferson. If convicted, Grace would not only lose her job, but even more distressing, she could be forced to forfeit her teaching certificate and possibly never be allowed to teach again.

The trial intensifies as Grace's defense attorney, Tom Endler, calls Lee Strobel and Detective J. Warner Wallace, two experts who have written on the authenticity of Jesus, to the witness stand. If the defense could establish the person of Jesus and the events in His life as historical fact, then Grace would be found legitimately teaching about Jesus as she would any other historical figure.

It's the jury's duty to examine the facts and weigh the evidence. The proof must be convincing, based on reason and common sense, and not based solely on speculation or mere conjecture. They must undergo a careful, impartial consideration of all the evidence, or lack thereof, and reach a verdict beyond a reasonable doubt.

But can the life of Jesus be proven beyond *a reasonable doubt*? Does any hard evidence really exist for the events in Jesus's life? If so, is it reliable? What about His death by crucifixion? And can His alleged resurrection be credible? Perhaps it's our duty to also examine, question, and test the evidence for the historical Jesus, and draw a conclusion one way or the other.

Meanwhile, another character in the film begins to investigate these very same questions. *God's Not Dead 2* zooms into sharp focus on the life of Brooke Thawley, the young student who raised the question about Jesus in Grace's class. We see Brooke somberly sitting alone in her brother's room. Workers had been walking in and out of the room, removing his belongings and loading them into a truck. Her brother died six months earlier, but in many ways it seems like yesterday. She can't believe he's really gone. The empty, barren room becomes an outward picture of her heart—and the constant ache in her chest. Life just doesn't make sense anymore.

One of the workers returns to hand her a book. "I found this among your brother's things. It seemed like it would be something you'd like to keep." Apparently, her brother was reading the Bible without Brooke knowing about it. Why didn't he tell her? Didn't he trust her? As she turns the pages, she discovers notes and markings in the margins of the Bible and wonders if he had been searching for something, some purpose to life, as she is now. Or had he already found what he was looking for?

SEARCHING FOR MEANING

In another classroom, in another country, many years earlier, Viktor Frankl was intently observing his science teacher walking up and down the rows of desks declaring, "Life is nothing! In the final analysis, life is nothing more than a combustion process, a process of oxidation." Thirteen-year-old Frankl jumped up out of his chair without asking permission, as was customary at the time, and replied, "What meaning, then, does life have?"[1]

Driven by that haunting question, Frankl went on to study psychological patterns and behaviors based on the pursuit of meaning. He proposed that finding meaning in life is humanity's primary motivation. The theories he subsequently developed are known as the third school of psychotherapy, after Freud's and Adler's theories.[2]

In 1942, Frankl had the opportunity to put his theories to the test. He was newly married, with his career just starting to take off, as the Nazis began rounding up the Jews in Vienna. Eventually, Frankl, along with his wife and parents, were transported to a concentration camp. He survived; his family did not. Three years after he was liberated, he wrote his magnum opus in nine days: the 1946 best seller *Man's Search for Meaning*, based on his dreadful experience in the concentration camp. It's become one of the most influential books of our time.[3]

Meaning is defined as something bigger than ourselves, regardless of our circumstances. Frankl wrote, "If there is any meaning in life at all, then there must be meaning in suffering."[4]

A central theme of Frankl's work is about finding or ascribing a meaning to our losses, our sufferings, our tragedies. When any of us experience pain, a very human reaction is to cry out, "Why? Why me? Why?" Frankl contended, "Those that have a 'why' to live can bear with almost any 'how.'"[5]

Out of the suffering he witnessed and experienced in that horrific concentration camp, Viktor Frankl found that he came away with a deeper faith, incredibly, in humanity and in God. We are designed at the very core of our beings, our souls, to long for something more.[6]

Many believe that designer is God, who invites us to seek Him out and discover meaning, as described in the Bible: "God did this so that they would seek him and perhaps reach out for him and find him, though he is not far from any one of us."[7]

Brooke's emptiness and heartache lead her to pour out her heart to her teacher, Grace, at a chance meeting in a coffee shop. "Why did my brother have to die? There's no reason. . . . I feel totally lost."

As Brooke opens up with her teacher, it's obvious she respects Grace very much. Finally, Brooke reaches a breaking point and blurts out, "How do you keep it together in spite of the challenges of life?"

Grace calmly gives her a one-word answer: "Jesus."

CHAPTER 1
WHY JESUS?

These are written that you may believe that Jesus is the Messiah, the Son of God, and that by believing you may have life in his name.

—John 20:31

“I’d like to talk to you about Jesus.” Is there anything more uncomfortable than someone you don’t know approaching you with that question? Stand-up comedian Jim Gaffigan raises this scenario in his comedy routine. He imagines his retort to that stranger: “Yeah, um, I’d like you to *not*!” Gaffigan jokes that even with some religious leaders, if you walked up to them on the street and said you wanted to talk about Jesus, they’d say, “Easy there, pal, I like to keep work at work. I’m not some freak! Make an appointment to catch me in the office, okay?”

While he uses humor to poke a little fun, Gaffigan brings to light just how powerful the name of Jesus is—it can clear a room or stop you in your tracks. When Jesus is first mentioned in the classroom scene in *God’s Not Dead 2*, one student’s reaction is to immediately text his parents, presumably accusing the teacher of inappropriately sharing her faith. However, Brooke’s reaction to hearing the name of Jesus mentioned in the coffee shop is quite different. Her curiosity is piqued, intensifying her search to find more information, discover answers to her questions, and uncover the truth about Jesus.

Why is Jesus a lightning rod for such strong reactions? Why has He created spirited controversy throughout history, from the first century when Jesus walked the earth until today? Although some perceive Jesus as meek and weak with a few nice things to say, the truth is He confronted the religious leaders of His day, was unafraid to stand counter to the culture, and did not waver when He clashed with Roman authorities. The cause behind all the controversy springs from the bold, audacious claims Jesus made. Not only that, the trouble intensifies when vast numbers of people actually believe Jesus's claims, devote their lives to Him, and are even willing to die for Him. Other historical figures have influenced and left their mark on the world, but the impact of Jesus over the last twenty centuries is unparalleled.

In the movie, the name of Jesus sets Brooke on a path toward a better understanding of what Jesus claimed, but it also begins the spiritual journey of Grace's lawyer, Tom. Initially, Tom took on the case for the sheer challenge of it! But as he delves further into his preparation for trial, Tom realizes that the facts about Jesus would play a major role in winning the case. And the more he learns about Jesus, the more passionate he becomes about knowing the truth surrounding Jesus's claims. This endeavor challenges his preconceived ideas—it quickly becomes personal! At one point, Grace hands him a book, *Man, Myth, Messiah: Answering History's Greatest Question*. The title refers to a question Jesus asked His disciples: "Who do you say I am?" It's a life-changing question because the answer is life changing. Grace knowingly pats Tom on his shoulder and says, "You've got a lot of reading to do!"

CLAIMS ABOUT GOD

Throughout history, people who paid attention to Jesus got their preconceived paradigms challenged and their lives transformed. For instance, Jesus claimed we could address God as "Our Father." This startled His listeners and broke away from centuries of tradition imagining God to be distant, very high up in His heaven, and the sort of God you wouldn't want to get too close to. If people could envision God as "Father," they would obtain a frame of reference regarding who God is that could reorient their relationship to Him.

If God is the Father, then we are the children. Jesus claimed we could experience a parent-child relationship with God. And we are invited to call the creator of heaven and earth "Our Father."

The implication is that God is not distant and uninvolved, but rather He is intimately interested. He cares. He hears. He loves. Just as a parent would care, guide, correct, discipline, and love his or her child, God desires to relate to us in a similar way. Now certainly, our relationship with our earthly parents isn't perfect, which can sometimes twist our understanding of what Jesus is really saying. Yet undoubtedly, there are few relationships that can either wreck us or bring deep, transformational love like our relationship with one of our parents. Jesus taught that God is the most consistent, loving Father one could possibly have.

Holding this image of a father in our minds is only one way of describing the depth of love, care, and concern God has for us. Jesus illustrated the nature of God and our relationship to Him through parables, which affirmed God's protection and provision. Jesus also claimed God's generosity is limitless, that He is relentless in His pursuit of us, and that He desires to be in right relationship with us.

CLAIMS ABOUT HIMSELF

If we made a list of the world's great religious leaders and compared what they said about connecting with God, a striking revelation comes into view.

First of all, it may come as a surprise that Jesus didn't claim to be a religious leader. He did the majority of His work of ministering to people outside of the established religious institutions. In some ways, He was against religion. Religious leaders of His day were, in fact, shocked at His lack of respect for their traditions. He seemed to have a habit of calling them out on their hypocrisy. Jesus knew that religion could be like a dangerous weight hanging overhead, and He wanted to set people free from its heavy burdens.

Secondly, the founders of other religions all had a message about how to live. They spoke about instructions and rules for getting along with others and getting right with God. They elaborated on how to religiously follow a right way of living. For example, Buddha pointed to the Noble Truths and offered this as the way to get aligned with the truth and achieve nirvana. Buddha distinctly made a point to say that he was a mere man, not a god. It is not Buddha to whom you *turn*; it is Buddha to whom you *listen*.[1]

On the other hand, Jesus's message time and again was all about following Him, that He Himself was the Way. He not only taught a right way of living, but He claimed He *embodied* the way to live rightly.[2] Jesus said that He did not come to abolish the Law or the Prophets, but instead came to fulfill them. In other words, He didn't just point to His message, He pointed to Himself. Jesus declared, "I am the way and the truth and the life. No one comes to the Father except through me."[3]

If that didn't shake up His listeners enough, Jesus also claimed He had the authority to forgive sins. When people heard this, their immediate response was to ask, "Who is this who even forgives sins?"[4] The religious leaders clearly understood the implication Jesus was making, because they knew only God could forgive sins.

"Anyone who has seen me has seen the Father,"[5] Jesus asserted. Then He removed all doubt as to what He meant when He stated plainly, "I and the Father are one. . . . Why then do you accuse me of blasphemy because I said, 'I am God's Son'?"[6] Here Jesus claimed to be the Son of God, and the people picked up rocks, ready to stone Him for saying such a thing.

On top of that, He boldly stated that it was through Him that we could receive everlasting life. He didn't merely say where people could go to find eternal life, but He declared that He, and only He, could provide eternal life. Jesus said, "I am the resurrection and the life. The one who believes in me will live, even though they die; and whoever lives by believing in me will never die."[7]

Do the claims of Jesus start to seem outrageous and far-fetched to you?

For many, these claims of Jesus are nothing short of good news. For instance, Desmond Tutu, Archbishop of Cape Town, said, "What a tremendous relief it is to discover that we don't need to prove ourselves to God. That is what Jesus came to say, and for that he got killed. He came to say, 'You don't have to earn God's love. It is not a matter of human achievement. You exist because God loves you already.' That is tremendous stuff—that is the Good News."[8]

Yet many people object that simply making outlandish claims in and of themselves does not make those claims true and real. In his early life, C. S. Lewis was very skeptical regarding the claims of Christianity. "Here comes the real shock," Lewis wrote in *Mere Christianity*. "Among these Jews there suddenly turns up a man who goes about talking as if He was God!"[9] Lewis expressed reluctance about Jesus's claims, even deeming Jesus was nothing more than a myth.

So, is there any real proof that Jesus was who He said He was? And what exactly determines the adequacy of that proof?

CHAPTER 2

WHAT IS TRUTH?

Do I still have to add that, in the entire New Testament, there is only one solitary figure one is obliged to respect? Pilate, the Roman governor.

—*Friedrich Nietzsche,* The Antichrist

What is truth?

—*Pilate, John 18:38*

How do you know that Abraham Lincoln was shot in a theater? Or that Marco Polo traveled through Asia and met the Kublai Khan? Or how do you know that the Chicago Cubs won the World Series in 1908?

Can you prove these events happened? How would you evaluate the evidence? Would you bring the data into a laboratory and put it under a microscope? Or enter the claims into a mathematical formula and come up with the answers? No, not everything can be determined in a scientific or mathematical arena. Just as it would be difficult to scientifically prove that you love your spouse, or how you celebrated your tenth birthday, or that you are a die-hard Cubs fan. However, these assertions could be verified using historical research and weighing the evidence in an appropriate manner.

Civilizations throughout the ages have established means for determining the truth of events and resolving issues involving conflicting accounts. Through logic and debate, expert testimony and witnesses, the court arrives at a resolution based on careful, impartial consideration of all the evidence or lack thereof.

A determination is reached, judgments rendered, and sentences carried out with life-altering results: a prisoner is released, a person's rights are forfeited, a parent is awarded custody of a child—or not! The burden of proof is of supreme importance; the court will not make these decisions unless the preponderance of evidence exists. In criminal cases, it must be proven beyond a reasonable doubt.

In *God's Not Dead 2*, the attorneys and the school administrators put a lot of stock in the court system's ability to determine the truth of their case—with the help of a civil liberties organization. The chief prosecuting attorney, Peter Kane, arrives on the scene exuding confidence in both the judicial system and their particular case. "How can we lose?" he seems to proclaim with a twinkle in his eye and a knowing, slightly smug smile. He's certain this will go down in the history books as a "landmark constitutional case concerning the separation of church and state!" Kane clearly believes the truth will win the day in court and it couldn't be more obvious to him that he's on the side of the "truth." With great self-satisfaction, he pronounces, "We are going to prove once and for all that God is dead."

GREENLEAF'S RULES OF EVIDENCE

For much of his life, Simon Greenleaf would have agreed with the attorneys in the movie. He was one of the chief founders of Harvard Law School and widely regarded as one of the brightest minds to have ever practiced the legal profession. He authored a three-volume classic, *A Treatise on the Law of Evidence,* which is considered to be "the greatest single authority on the rules for evidence in the entire literature of legal procedure."[1]

Greenleaf was an agnostic, believing Christianity to be a hoax or, at best, a childish fairy tale. The professor often derided students he discovered to be followers of Jesus. He would speak openly in the classroom about how foolish and unenlightened people would need to be to believe in Jesus Christ. But then one day, his students stood up to him with a challenge to apply the same rules of evidence administered in the court of justice to the claims of Christianity. Specifically, they dared him to examine the "resurrection myth" since he often referred to it in such a dismissive manner.

Greenleaf eagerly took up the challenge and set out on what he predicted to be another typical open-and-shut case. However, in the process of trying to refute and discredit the Resurrection, he discovered to his amazement that the preponderance of evidence pointed to it as an actual occurrence, and not fiction. Greenleaf then turned his legal mind to the events found in the Gospels of Matthew, Mark, Luke, and John. Here he created a lengthy list of observations and conclusions that he compiled in a now-famous apologetic essay with a similarly lengthy title: *The Testimony of the Evangelists Examined by the Rules of Evidence Administered in the Courts of Justice.*

Each of Greenleaf's arguments is worth contemplating, since they convincingly conclude that the Gospels are reliable and accurate accounts of actual events. Three notable points stand out from his essay:

1. The existing copies of the original Gospels (the originals are not known to exist) are at least as authentic and reliable as any other works of antiquity; the Gospel accounts would be admissible as evidence and would hold up in court.

2. The testimonies within the Gospels demonstrate consistencies that support the credibility of the witnesses. The paradoxes between the testimonies are plausible and enhance their veracity.

3. The ancient documents outside the Gospels by other known writers of the time (Tacitus, Josephus, Seutonius, etc.) contain supporting evidence admissible in court and corroborate the findings in the Gospel accounts.[2]

After careful scrutiny of the evidence, the distinguished Greenleaf concluded that the most reasonable position to hold is that Jesus lived and died and resurrected. With that, he committed himself to follow Jesus for the rest of his life.

A year before he died, Greenleaf wrote to the American Bible Society: "Of the Divine character of the Bible, I think no man who deals honestly with his own mind and heart can entertain a reasonable doubt. For myself, I must say, that having for many years made the evidences of Christianity the subject of close study, the result has been a firm and increasing conviction of the authenticity and plenary inspiration of the Bible. It is indeed the Word of God."[3]

A major turning point in *God's Not Dead 2* happens when Grace's lawyer, Tom, has a heart to heart with her about the status of the trial. It isn't looking like they are going to win. The fact remains that Grace did talk about Jesus in the classroom, citing verses from the Bible, which could be interpreted as sharing her faith and blurring the lines that separate church and state.

"But this isn't about faith! This is about history!" Grace declares. "It's about the facts!"

"Yes, that's the problem," Tom agrees. "You talked about Jesus and His teachings as if they were a verifiable fact."

"And what if they are just that: historical facts?" she argues. "I didn't do it in a physics class or a science laboratory. It didn't happen in calculus. I teach history where it's all about the facts. Just because those facts happen to be recorded in a faith tradition doesn't mean they stop being the facts."

Tom's face lights up. "Grace, that's it! That's our case! Jesus existed, as an actual historical person. I love it!"

If Tom could establish by a preponderance of the evidence that Jesus actually lived, and demonstrate proof in a court of law that the events surrounding Jesus's life are verifiable, then their whole case could be won. He sets off to examine the evidence for himself—but where does one begin?

Simon Greenleaf would suggest, according to the Rules for Evidence, that the search starts with "a mind free from all pride of opinion, not hostile to the truth, willing to pursue . . . impartiality to weigh the arguments and evidence, and to acquiesce in the judgment of right reason."[4] In other words, we begin with an open mind and objective approach, allowing the historical facts to lead us to the truth.

CHAPTER 3

WAS JESUS REAL?

An unbelieved truth can hurt a man much more than a lie. It takes great courage to back truth unacceptable to our times. There's a punishment for it, and it's usually crucifixion. —*John Steinbeck,* East of Eden

"We acknowledge Jesus every time we write the date. In fact, this very court affirms Jesus as a real person when we were called into session!" Lee Strobel begins his testimony with a bang.

A compelling *God's Not Dead 2* scene unfolds when Grace's attorney calls two expert witnesses to the stand to testify to the evidence of the historical Jesus. If the attorney can establish a credible proof of the life of Jesus, then Grace will have been vindicated in discussing Jesus in her history class. Strobel, a best-selling author and professor, has several jury members chuckling as they catch the irony of his opening reference. He clarifies that our calendar is divided into BC and AD based on the birth of Jesus. "That's quite an accomplishment for someone if he never even existed!" he quips.

Then Strobel boldly states that we know Jesus existed beyond all reasonable doubt. Scholars, he explains, have identified more than thirty-nine ancient sources for Jesus from which derive more than one hundred reported facts about His life, teachings, crucifixion, and resurrection. These sources include records from outside of the New Testament Bible. For example, the Jewish historian Flavius Josephus recorded events on behalf of the Roman authorities during the time of Jesus. He was not biased toward the growing Christian movement. Yet Josephus, along with other extrabiblical sources such as the writings of Tacitus, Pliny the younger, Lucian of Samosata, and the Babylonian Talmud, confirms various facts about Jesus. They report that Jesus was revered as a teacher, was regarded as wise, gathered a following, had a brother named James, was crucified, and that, remarkably, a large number of people continued to worship Him!

It's fascinating to note that these ancient historians had to determine the validity of an event or occurrence by using multiple sources themselves.[1] Today, a majority of historical scholars recognize these basic details in the life of Jesus as reliable and trustworthy based on this overwhelming source material. "By comparison," Strobel ascertains, "we have better evidence for Jesus's life than we have for Alexander the Great conquering the known world!"

Strobel's burst of information is momentarily interrupted by an assertion that his testimony is most certainly biased because he admittedly is a Christian. But Strobel counters that for most of his life he was an atheist. He believed the notion of an all-powerful, all-knowing God was ridiculous and the idea that Jesus was the Son of God, ludicrous!

A JOURNALIST'S ASSESSMENT OF A LIFE

Both Lee Strobel and Detective J. Warner Wallace play themselves in the movie—not fictional characters—and reveal their real-life, personal stories of wrestling with the evidence of Christianity on a journey from atheism to belief and full devotion. They uncovered the truth in the historical records concerning Jesus, and it changed the course of their lives. They became believers in Christ.

Strobel has a background in journalism and law. Extremely skeptical by nature, he was a court reporter, legal editor, and journalist at the *Chicago Tribune* for fourteen years. He demanded hard evidence before he would believe something—anything. But when his wife began to explore spiritual things and eventually became a follower of Jesus Christ, Strobel thought his marriage was over, that she'd gotten involved in some kind of cult, and he wanted no part of it. Yet over time, he noticed subtle, and some not-so-subtle, changes occurring in her, in her demeanor, in the way she related to their children, and in how she interacted with him. That triggered in him an all-out quest to get to the bottom of this "Christian hoax." Deep in his heart, he knew that if Christianity turned out to be valid and credible, his life would never be the same.[2]

Using his journalism and legal skills, he thoroughly investigated the claims of Jesus for more than twenty-one months. His conclusion was undeniable. Given the massive amount of evidence, he determined it would take "more faith for him to remain an atheist than for him to believe in the claims of Jesus."[3] He couldn't remain indifferent; he was trained to go wherever the evidence took him. And that trail pointed him to the truth of Jesus Christ.[4]

"No, the facts do not change even if there was a bias on my part," Strobel continues from the witness stand. "We have non-Christian sources and we have agnostic scholars with no sympathy toward Christianity who affirm the events of Jesus."

Strobel concludes his testimony by quoting Bart Ehrman, an agnostic professor at UNC Chapel Hill: "I am not a Christian, but as an historian I think evidence matters. And the past matters. And for anyone to whom both evidence and the past matter, a dispassionate consideration of the case makes it plain: Jesus did exist."

A DETECTIVE'S ANALYSIS

Next, the defense calls to the stand J. Warner Wallace, a homicide detective specializing in cold cases. These are cases where the events happened in the distant past and typically no eyewitnesses are alive. In fact, these cases have gone cold because there is little or no direct evidence associated with the case. Contrary to the popular TV shows, most cold cases do not get solved through DNA or other laboratory procedures. Rather, these types of cases are solved through Forensic Statement Analysis, the careful examination of testimony taken years earlier, at the time of the crime. Wallace is an expert in the process of inspecting the related past statements, making comparisons, finding correlations; identifying emphasis versus omissions or minimizations; and separating *apparent* inconsistencies from *actual* inconsistencies.[5]

Wallace had been a vocal atheist, but at the age of thirty-five he turned his attention to analyzing the case for Christianity. At first, he focused on the death and burial of Jesus, which was, after all, a homicide at the hands of the Romans. Utilizing parallels from his years of police work investigating crimes and examining evidence, Wallace concluded that the Gospels are, indeed, direct eyewitness accounts of the life of Jesus. It's "the same sort of testimony that we consider the best-of-all-possible evidence in a court of law," Wallace adds as he turns to the jury, "across all four Gospels."

The prosecuting attorney protests that the consistency among all four Gospels is due to a conspiracy. But Wallace retorts that, in the event of a conspiracy, the accounts would appear either much *more* alike, or much *less*. "When witnesses have time to compare notes and 'get their stories straight,' then they rehearse an exact retelling of the same events with the same details, using the very same wording," Wallace explains. "There's no deviation. It's a dead giveaway."

"And if they have just a general goal of lying and they're fabricating the events out of thin air, the accounts will differ wildly with all sorts of inconsistencies," Wallace continues. "But the four Gospels are four distinctly different recountings of the same events. They might be told in different fashions, but that's how real-life testimony of actual eyewitnesses functions.

"Think about this example: If a head-on collision occurs in traffic, several eyewitness accounts will emerge with a variety of different details, but the fact that the collision was head-on will remain," Wallace says. "Or take the night before His crucifixion, when Jesus appeared before the high priest Caiaphas, Matthew's Gospel recounts Jesus getting taunted, with those who slapped Him shouting, 'Prophesy to us! Who is the one hitting you?' This would seem to be an odd question to ask since His attackers are standing right there in front of Him. However, Luke's Gospel reveals that Jesus was blindfolded, so given this context, the question raised in Matthew makes more sense. An instance of how one Gospel account supports the other unintentionally."[6]

Implementing his skills as a detective, Wallace attests that the various biblical and nonbiblical accounts are written in a manner that mirrors what would be expected of independent eyewitnesses accurately describing what actually happened.[7] To put it plainly, the stories corroborate. They ring true!

Wallace pauses to look each member of the jury in the eye. "Let me sum this all up for you. After years of intense study, I consider the four Gospels of this book," holding up the Bible, he continues, "to contain a series of eyewitness accounts authenticating the actual words of Jesus, not only when and where He said them, but to whom and for what purpose."

The attentive jury sits in silence for a moment, considering the implications of all the evidence that has been presented so far: expert analysis from both a detective and a journalist, historical data compared, eyewitness accounts corroborated, and a robust logic articulated. Even scholars critical of Jesus were cited, such as John Dominic Crossan of the Jesus Seminar, who concludes "that [Jesus] was crucified is as sure as anything historical can ever be."[8]

And yet, even if a preponderance of evidence proves beyond a reasonable doubt that Jesus was historical; that He existed; that He spoke the words recorded in the Gospels; and that He made those audacious claims, and was even crucified and died because of them—that still may not mean He was who He claimed to be. People have made claims all throughout history, but their words could be nothing but nonsense, or empty lies.

So, is there any evidence that can verify that the historical Jesus was who He claimed to be? Is there anything that could demonstrate His words are true once and for all?

Fortunately, there was an event that does just that—and it changed everything.

My old assumptions about how the world works are buried, yet my new ones aren't yet operational. There's been a death of sorts, but without a few days in hell, no resurrection is possible.

—*Mary Karr,* Lit

CHAPTER 4

DOES JESUS MATTER?

"Who are these people? I never heard of them!"

Lionel Luckhoo's secretary held up the invitation. "It's from the Full Gospel Business Men's Fellowship International."

"Too long of a name! Too cumbersome!" Luckhoo grumbled. "I'm tired out before you finish telling me. I'm certainly not going to that dinner!"

Sir Lionel Luckhoo is recognized as the "world's most successful attorney of all time" in the *Guinness Book of World Records* for having obtained the largest number of successive murder acquittals. No one has ever come near his record of procuring a "not guilty" verdict 245 consecutive times. Luckhoo holds other remarkable distinctions: twice knighted by Queen Elizabeth II of England, and one of only a few to have ever served as an Ambassador of two sovereign nations simultaneously.

Luckhoo never had any intention of going to such a dinner, but three hours before the event, a Full Gospel representative called to ask if he was planning to be there. Their worldwide organization was setting up a chapter in Luckhoo's hometown in Guyana and their only agenda was to meet up over a meal to discuss Jesus and "to invite others to meet Jesus."

"I already know all about Jesus," Luckhoo remarked impatiently. "Listen, I have the inquisitive mind of a defense attorney, so rest assured that I have examined the available written testimonies and weighed the multiple evidences. I have no doubt Jesus was an historical figure, who certainly made some outrageous claims and clearly made a significant mark in history. So I'm not your target audience."

The representative simply replied, "You can know about Jesus without knowing Jesus."

Luckhoo went silent on the phone. It struck a chord of truth in him.

"I must be able to raise questions. I have a suspicious mind—you don't have a career in law without being skeptical." Luckhoo attempted to gauge their level of receptivity to engage in dialogue with doubters. "Your meeting is at a hotel banquet room, correct? If it were held at a church, I would not be going."

When Luckhoo arrived, he met people from various walks of life. The discussion was authentic, allowing for, and even encouraging, healthy debate. As the subject matter narrowed to the resurrection of Jesus, Luckhoo was riveted. Moreover, the countenance of those around him reflected a quiet joy and peace that aroused his curiosity and captured his attention. Just before guests were dismissed, the facilitator welcomed everyone who wanted to stay and pray with someone to walk to the front corner of the room.

Luckhoo scanned the room and noticed many people whom he actually knew personally. Everything inside of him wanted to walk forward to pray, but he hesitated. "I'd been the mayor of my hometown. I was one of the respected leaders of my country, and peer pressure caused me to wobble," he would later explain. "And yet, I saw they had something I wanted."[1]

In that moment, he reflected back on his life. "Everything had gone my way. I had everything. I had a little bit of education, a little bit of money, a little bit of culture, and a little bit of honor. I had enjoyed a number of successes. Everything was running smoothly for me. And yet I found I didn't have peace. It was something I couldn't understand, but during that time over several months, I couldn't sleep at night. I wrestled in my bed, tossing and turning. If I could have purchased peace, I would have written a blank check! I thought, I wasn't a bad man, I hadn't done anything terribly wrong, yet I had no peace and I couldn't understand it."[2]

He sat there in his seat mesmerized, unable to leave. He was overwhelmed with the sense that his spiritual state was like fallow ground, a dry and barren soil, strewn with weeds. By contrast, looking into the faces of the men at this gathering, he saw fertile spiritual soil with abundant growth. He perceived a peace in them—something he had always longed for but had never obtained. "And it seemed as though Jesus Himself was knocking at the door of my heart, bidding me to open to Him."[3] Luckhoo got up and slowly walked to the front corner of the room to pray, and right then and there he began a process that would completely transform his life.

Later that night, when he arrived home, he performed what he described as a *"post mortem"* on what had happened at the meeting. This launched him into a thorough and complete investigation of the life of Jesus, focusing mainly on the Resurrection. After all, it is on this momentous event that the whole of the Christian faith stands or crumbles.

EVIDENCE OF RESURRECTION

As *God's Not Dead 2* illustrates, the historian's task is very much like that of a trial lawyer. The witnesses' accounts are matched and analyzed to re-create the course of events. In the case of the Resurrection, referenced more than three hundred times in the Bible, it's not surprising that it had a dramatic impact on the lives of Jesus's followers. After some initially denied being His disciples, they later boldly and vehemently declared that they had encountered the risen Jesus. As acclaimed historian Paula Fredriksen has demonstrated, this is one of the most striking facts recognized even by skeptics of the Resurrection:

> *I know in their own terms what they saw was the raised Jesus. That's what they say, and then all the historic evidence we have afterwards attests to their conviction that that's what they saw. I'm not saying that they really did see the raised Jesus. I wasn't there. I don't know what they saw. But I do know as an historian that they must have seen something.*[4]

On the Sunday following the Crucifixion, Jesus's tomb was found empty by a group of His women followers. Their testimony is especially significant because the testimony of women during that era was not even acceptable in a court of law. No one would have deliberately chosen women to establish the validity of the empty tomb, since it would have been considered embarrassing to rely on their testimony as proof. This, therefore, presents good reason to accept their accounts as authentic.

And the story itself is told in a remarkably straightforward and restrained manner. Even though the Resurrection was not directly witnessed by anyone, the account is not embellished with imagery or figurative language, which suggests the event is not a legend. Additionally, according to the disciples' reports, the body was no longer in the tomb, which corroborates the Jewish accusations that the disciples had stolen the body. They made these allegations because the body was, in fact, missing.

Finally, one of the strongest arguments for the credibility of Jesus's resurrection is that many of His disciples were sentenced to death for proclaiming that Jesus arose, yet none recanted his story to save his life. Think about this: Many die for something they believe to be true, but no one dies for a story they know to be a lie.

"I approached the resurrection from the point of view of a lawyer," Luckhoo said. "We are confronted with these evidences beyond recall, beyond probabilities as in a civil case, or beyond a reasonable doubt as in a criminal case. I tell you plainly, it is beyond a shadow of a doubt. Jesus did rise from the dead. And because of that, there's hope for the world."[5]

The miracle of the resurrection of Jesus affirms His audacious, life-changing claims. It undeniably declares with power and authority that Jesus was who He said He was, the Son of the living God. This is the very heart of the Gospel.

Later in his life, Luckhoo wrote something well worth pondering today: "It is the greatest case I have ever pleaded and I am confident, because all the evidence is on our side. The verdict must be that Jesus is Lord, and that He is coming back soon to proclaim His people 'not guilty' and to take us to be with Him forever."[6]

EPILOGUE

Believing in him is not the same as believing things about him such as that he was born of a virgin and raised Lazarus from the dead. Instead, it is a matter of giving our hearts to him, of come hell or high water putting our money on him, the way a child believes in a mother or a father, the way a mother or a father believes in a child. —*Frederick Buechner*

"We call Grace Wesley to the stand!"

Grace is taken aback! This was not the agreed-upon plan. Grace was not supposed to have to defend herself on the witness stand. Tom's defense strategy was to demonstrate beyond reasonable doubt the historicity of Jesus and His claims, in order to win the case against her for teaching about Jesus in her history class. What's happening here? *God's Not Dead 2* takes a sharp turn, indeed!

"Grace, I want you to apologize," her attorney says, not wasting any time.

Grace is dumbfounded.

"I want you to say you're sorry . . . tell them you made a mistake," Tom says.

"I can't do that," she responds.

"Why?" Tom asks.

Grace glances at the packed courtroom. "Because . . . I don't believe I did anything wrong," she manages to mumble.

"As your attorney, I'm advising you to do it anyway." Tom implores her to consider the trouble she is causing for herself. It's really unnecessary, he seems to suggest, and invites her to retract her words and be done with this mess. For a moment, Grace appears tempted to make it all go away with a simple denial. "At least pretend that you're sorry—and throw yourself on the mercy of the court—" Tom continues.

Grace cuts him off: "That would be a lie."

"So what? Everyone lies," says Tom.

"Not everyone," responds Grace.

"Then what is it you want, Grace?" Tom asks.

What does she want? His question reverberates through Grace's mind. She wants to get back on track and prove her case with the preponderance of evidence that Jesus was real. Wasn't that the plan? Wasn't that going to be enough to win the case? How could things have gotten so far off the rails? After all, it was just an ordinary, respectable history class, she recalls, when a student raised a simple, honest question and she merely responded with an honest answer—the truth of Jesus. She can't retract it, she concludes, nor can she apologize. It would be denying the truth.

"I want to be able to tell the truth," she finally responds.

"The truth? *Whose* truth? What truth are you referring to?" Tom asks. "Grace, is there some truth that you know . . . ? Oh, that's right! The other night, didn't you admit . . ."

Immediately Grace knows what Tom is referencing. Just the other night, she had revealed to him the question she felt God brought to her mind in a watershed moment in her life. And here on the witness stand she is certain what he is going after now—the same pivotal question: "Who is it that *you* say Jesus is?"

It is as if time stops in that moment in that courtroom. Grace slowly gazes over at the jury members' expectant faces. She notices everyone, including the prosecuting attorney, is leaning forward with anticipation. Then she spots Brooke in the crowd.

Grace can't help but think back to their time in the coffee shop, when Brooke was grieving her brother's death and searching for "something more to life." Grace tried to assure Brooke then that everyone who ever existed seeks after something more, a bigger purpose—meaning. But Brooke persisted and urged Grace to tell her what that "something more" was for her. Grace responded simply, "Jesus." And with one word, a whole sequence of events was set in motion.

Grace catches Brooke's eye and recalls the occasion when Brooke had raised her hand in class to ask about Jesus. Brooke was determined to find out why Jesus was so transforming. She read through the pages of her brother's Bible, hoping to discover for herself what Jesus said and did. His claims were so extraordinary; she knew in her heart that if they were true, they would be totally life altering. But how could she know if those claims were true?

Grace turns to her attorney, Tom. He is wholeheartedly convinced that the trial system is the most effective determiner of historical fact in civilization. Using objective reasoning and careful, impartial analysis of all the evidence, the court can arrive at the truth. Grace remembers how eager Tom was to bring the legal process to bear on the life of Jesus.

Grace anticipates addressing the members of the jury, gently, she hopes, yet confidently. It's in this moment she realizes that more than presenting all the evidence for Jesus, and lining up all the historical facts, the truth of the matter ultimately strikes home when a person takes a stand on that very question: "Who is Jesus?"

She recognizes this is one of the most important questions she has ever faced in her life. And she believes it's truly one we must all consider sooner or later. Jesus asked this question of His disciples, and He asks this of us today: "Who do you say I am?"

It's a life-changing question because the answer is life changing.

Finally, Grace answers, "He is the Christ, the Son of the living God."

As the story of *God's Not Dead 2* unfolds, the events surrounding the trial linger. It is as if the jury is still out regarding the question that Jesus asks of us: "Who do you say I am?" It is as if we have also heard the facts and witnessed for ourselves the expert testimonies. Perhaps we may need to delve further into the arguments and reasoning, but the process of weighing the evidence remains. It is as if the judge turns to each of us in the jury seats and gives his final instructions in the most clear and sincere manner: "Members of the jury, the time has now come when the great burden of reaching a just, fair, and conscientious decision in this case is to be thrown wholly upon you, the jurors selected for this important duty."

Now you must set aside your bias, step away from your preconceived ideas, and have the courage to allow the historical data to lead you to the truth. The credibility of the life of Jesus, the claims He has made, the actions He has taken, and all their implications offer significant transformational meaning to your life. The time is now to give an answer: Who do you say Jesus is?

The verdict is yours to render.

Once to every man and nation, comes the moment to decide, in the strife of truth with falsehood, for the good or evil side; some great cause, some great decision, offering each the bloom or blight, and the choice goes by forever, 'twixt that darkness and that light.

—James Russell Lowell

Look for Christ, and you will find Him, and with Him everything else.

—C. S. Lewis, Mere Christianity

NOTES

Introduction

1 Viktor Frankl, *The Unheard Cry for Meaning* (New York: Simon & Schuster, 1978), 41.

2 Viktor Frankl, *Man's Search for Meaning* (Boston: Beacon Press, 1959).

3 Listed according to the Library of Congress and the Book-of-the-Month Club as tied in 9th place: www.nytimes.com/1991/11/20/books/book-notes-059091.html.

4 Frankl, *Man's Search for Meaning.*

5 Frankl, *Man's Search for Meaning.*

6 Matthew Scully, "Viktor Frankl at 90: An Interview," *First Things*, April 1995, http://www.firstthings.com/article/1995/04/004-viktor-frankl-at-ninety-an-interview.

7 Acts 17:27.

Chapter 1: Why Jesus?

1 Ravi Zacharias, *Jesus Among Other Gods* (Nashville, TN: Word, 2000), 89, as referenced in *Is Jesus God,* article from y-jesus.com, http://y-jesus.com/wwrj/3-is-jesus-god/.

2 Zacharias.

3 John 14:6.

4 Luke 7:49.

5 John 14:9.

6 John 10:30,36.

7 John 11:25–26.

8 Christopher H. K. Persaud, *Famous People Speak About Jesus* (Xlibris Corp, 2004), 354.

9 C. S. Lewis, *Mere Christianity* (San Francisco: Harper, 2001), 51.

Chapter 2: What Is Truth?

1 Knott, *The Dictionary of American Biography*, as referenced on the back cover of Simon Greenleaf, *The Testimony of the Evangelists* (Grand Rapids, MI: Kregel Classics, 1995).

2 Greenleaf.

3 Stephen Abbott Northrop, ed., *A Cloud of Witnesses: The Greatest Men in the World for Christ* (American Heritage Ministries, 1987), 198.

4 Greenleaf, 5.

Chapter 3: Was Jesus Real?

1 *God's Not Dead 2 Study Guide* (Colorado Springs, CO: Outreach, 2016).

2 Lee Strobel, *The Case for Christ* (Grand Rapids, MI: Zondervan, 1998).

3 Strobel.

4 Strobel.

5 J. Warner Wallace, *Cold-Case Christianity* (Colorado Springs, CO: David C. Cook, 2013).

6 See Matthew 26:64–67; Luke 22:64.

7 *God's Not Dead 2 Study Guide.*

8 John Dominic Crossan, *Jesus: A Revolutionary Biography* (New York: HarperOne, 1995), 145.

Chapter 4: Does Jesus Matter?

1 Fred Archer, *Sir Lionel* (Gift Publications, 1980). See also Sir Lionel Luckhoo, *The Silent Witness* (Nashville, TN: Thomas Nelson, 1995).

2 Archer. See also Sir Lionel Luckhoo, "A Humble Ambassador for God," audiotape transcript, http://www.dayton-fgbmfi.org/luckhoo02.htm.

3 Archer.

4 Paula Fredriksen, interview with Peter Jennings in *The Search for Jesus*, ABC (June 26, 2000).

5 Archer; Luckhoo, "A Humble Ambassador."

6 Archer; Luckhoo, "A Humble Ambassador."

Tauwasser

Von

Prinz Emil von Schoenaich-Carolath

Berlin und Leipzig
G. J. Göschen'sche Verlagshandlung G. m. b. H.

Tauwasser

Tauwasser

Von

Prinz Emil von Schoenaich-Carolath

Vierte Auflage

Berlin und Leipzig
G. J. Göschen'sche Verlagshandlung G. m. b. H.
1912

Druck von Jul. Brandstätter (Inh. Gg. Neumann), Leipzig

Pellegrino del ciel', bel astro romito,
Che in prima giovinezza amai,
Ove t'aggiri adesso, e su qual lito
Piovi i tuoi rai? — — —

Er hieß Bent Sörensen, war ältester Sohn des Pastors Sörensen auf Mandergaard und studierte Mathematik in einer großen norddeutschen Stadt. Er war zwanzig Jahre alt, sehr schlank, weder hübsch noch häßlich, dafür aber ungewöhnlich langweilig. Er saß genau sechs Stunden im Kolleg und sechs Stunden bei seinen Büchern, obwohl er meist mit seinem Pensum viel früher fertig wurde. Wenn die Zeit um war, zog er eine Art von Überrock an und ging hinüber zu seiner Hauswirtin, um ihr anzuzeigen, daß er das Haus verlasse (als er noch auf der Schule war, hatte er sich beim Vater allabendlich melden müssen, wenn seine Arbeiten beendigt waren — nun hatte er das so aus Gewohnheit beibehalten); dann zog er ein Paar gestrickte Handschuhe an, setzte eine Mütze auf und ging bedächtig immer durch dieselben Straßen in ein Lokal, wo Studenten, Referendare, jüngere Künstler und angehende Doktoren zusammenzukommen pflegten. Dort angelangt, bot er schüchtern guten Abend, setzte sich ans unterste Ende des Tisches und ließ sich ein Glas Bier geben. Der Unterhaltung folgte er, besonders wenn sie ein wissenschaftliches Thema berührte, mit großer Aufmerksamkeit, beteiligte sich aber nur selten daran. Wenn die Uhr auf zehn ging, bezahlte er seine Zeche, grüßte, indem er den Oberkörper kurz und gewaltsam vorwärts stieß, und kehrte nach Hause zurück.

Es war unzweifelhaft, daß er sich an jenen Abenden vortrefflich unterhielt, dennoch gab es zwei Dinge, die ihm seinen stillen Genuß verkümmern konnten. Den oberen Platz der Stammtafel hatte ein junger Mann inne, welcher als angehender Dichter bekannt war und dessen Name in den Zeitschriften des Landes bereits genannt zu werden begann. Dieses liebenswürdige und talentvolle Tafelmitglied war für Bent ein Gegenstand heimlichen Grauens, er konnte nie verstehen, wie ein vernünftiges Wesen auch nur einen Bruchteil der kostbaren Zeit mit etwas so Unnützem und Systemlosem, wie ihm das Dichten erschien, vergeuden könne. Der Vorschlag, irgendwelche Reime zu ersinnen, hätte ihn angemutet wie eine Aufforderung, Seifenblasen in die Luft zu treiben, anstatt ins Kolleg zu gehen. Geschah es, daß auf Bitten der Gesellschaft der junge Mann Verse vortrug, so bemächtigte sich Bents eine große Unruhe, er sah betrübt nach der Uhr, welche die gesetzmäßige Zeit des Aufbruchs noch nicht anzeigte, und suchte unbemerkt zu entkommen. Sehr peinlich war es ihm auch, wenn man ihn veranlassen wollte, ein zweites Glas Bier zu bestellen. Er wurde dann meistens verlegen, stammelte einige unzusammenhängende Entschuldigungen und empfahl sich. Zu Hause angelangt, nahm er irgend eine Arbeit vor, um die Zeit bis zum Schlafengehen nicht unbenützt verstreichen zu lassen; dabei geschah es zuweilen, daß er sich in eintretende Schwierigkeiten verbiß und weder zu Bett, noch ins Kolleg ging, ehe sein Ziel erreicht und eine einfache, glatte

Lösung gefunden war. „Der junge Sörensen ist ein zäher, nüchterner Mensch, er wird es weit bringen", äußerte einmal gesprächsweise ein Professor. Ein Kollege, der zugegen war, meinte: „Damit bin auch ich einverstanden, allein wie sollte man nicht fleißig sein, wenn man die Stütze einer großen und gänzlich unbemittelten Familie ist? Ihm ist der Fleiß nicht so hoch anzurechnen wie anderen, die geringere Verpflichtungen besitzen." Der Herr Professor hatte einen vornehmen Studenten in Pension, welcher sich durch Faulheit und Liederlichkeit auszeichnete.

Bent Sörensen studierte in seinem vierten Semester. Daß der Winter zu Ende ging, merkte er nur daran, daß es in seinem Zimmer sehr kalt wurde, denn Frau Bitterlich, die Hauswirtin, pflegte von Mitte Februar ab nicht mehr einzuheizen. Bent stimmte ihr bei, denn er sah ein, daß System in ihrem Verfahren läge; er hatte außerdem nicht viel Zeit zum Frieren, denn er arbeitete unausgesetzt an einer verwickelten Nutzeffektberechnung, die er für einen Maschinenbauer aufstellen und für welche er acht Taler erhalten sollte. Er hatte sie in Abschnitte eingeteilt und erledigte jeden Tag unnachsichtlich sein Pensum; ganz am Ende, als er eben todmüde die Feder weglegen wollte, fand er, daß irgend etwas nicht einfach genug sei und kürzer ausgedrückt werden könne. Die dazu nötigen Formeln ergaben sich nicht sogleich, was für ihn Grund genug war, unbarmherzig bis in den Morgen hinein zu arbeiten. Er war fast am Ziele, als er eines Buches bedurfte, welches wegen Mangel an Raum nebst mehreren anderen in einer Kiste auf dem Hausboden verwahrt wurde. Diesen hatte er seit dem Tage, da er, von seinem Vater begleitet, bei Frau Bitterlich eingezogen war, nie mehr betreten, denn es lag dort planlos viel Gerümpel aufgestapelt und er haßte die Unordnung; jetzt aber bat er sich bei der Frau, die mit hochrotem Gesicht in der Küche umherhantierte, den Schlüssel aus und trat seine Wanderung an.

Weit war sie nicht. Das Haus hatte zwar fünf Stockwerke, allein Bents Zimmer lag, von der Straße aus gerechnet, bereits im vierten. Ganz oben wohnte ein Schneidermeister, der mußte ein ganz absonderlicher Geselle sein. Die Tür seiner Wohnung stand weit offen, er saß am Fenster auf einem Tische und nähte, dabei lachte er jedoch unaufhörlich; seine Frau schälte Kartoffeln und lachte auch, zwei rotbackige, ziemlich mangelhaft bekleidete Kinder wälzten sich am Boden und schrien vor Vergnügen, ein kleiner, unbeholfener Hund beteiligte sich am Konzerte, und in das Ganze warf ein goldgelber Kanarienvogel seine schmetternden Triller. Bent mißfiel diese Fröhlichkeit sehr, es kam ihm vor, als sei er in der Fremde. Hastig erstieg er die schmale hölzerne Treppe und schloß die Bodentür auf, eine dumpfe, auffallend warme Luft schlug ihm entgegen. Er fand sein Buch und wollte die Rückreise antreten, aber Luftwechsel und Übermüdung fielen plötzlich auf ihn, ihn überkam eine Schwäche und er mußte sich auf die Kiste setzen, den Kopf ans Gebälk legend. Nach einer Minute ward ihm besser, er bedurfte aber frischer Luft und bemühte sich, eins der schweren Dachfenster zu öffnen. Dies gelang ihm nicht, dagegen bemerkte er eine schmale Tür, die ins Freie führen mußte und nur durch einen Holzriegel geschlossen war. Sie gab dem Drucke seiner Hand leicht nach, ein Lichtstrom brach in den dämmernden Raum, so voll und blendend, daß er die Hand über die Augen legte, ein frischer Windstoß brauste um seine Stirne, er tat halb unbewußt einen Schritt vorwärts.

Eine angstvolle Stimme schlug an sein Ohr, sie rief einige wilde Worte in fremder Sprache. Er öffnete die Augen und sah unter sich einen Abgrund, Straßen, die sich kreuzten, finstere Höfe und rauchende Schlote. Hart neben ihm, auf einem platten Dache, zwischen Blumentöpfen und grünenden Gewächsen stand ein junges Mädchen und sah ihn mit großen Augen an. Sie war ohne Hut, nur in einen Schal von feinem Gewebe gehüllt, der Wind fing sich darin und wehte ihn fester um die schlanke Gestalt. Bent trat instinktmäßig, um nicht zu fallen, aufs Dach herüber und klammerte sich fest ans Geländer ... ob sie zu ihm sprach, wußte er nicht, aber sie sah nicht unfreundlich aus und betrachtete ihn unverwandt; das gab ihm den Mut, irgend etwas zu sagen, wovon nur die Worte „Vergebung" und „wäre es möglich ... ein Glas Wasser ..." deutlich herauskamen. Dann tat es ihm fast leid, daß er gesprochen hatte, denn sie wandte sich ab, sprang ein paar niedrige Stufen hinunter und verschwand, allerdings nur auf einen Augenblick, denn sie erschien sofort wieder und reichte ihm ein hastig gefülltes Glas, von dessen Wandung die eisigen Tropfen rannen.

„Warum wollten Sie sterben?“ frug sie sanft und mit sehr fremdartiger Betonung.

Er antwortete nicht und trank tiefatmend das kühle Wasser, es wurde ihm rasch besser, nur starrte er noch ein wenig traumbefangen vor sich hin. Der Märzwind stieß über die Dächer, die Sonne schien zum erstenmal und vor ihm stand das junge Mädchen mit den fragenden Augen und der blassen Stirn, um die das weiche Haar dunkel und küssend wehte.

„Ich wollte nicht sterben“, sagte er endlich schüchtern. „Ich bin nur heraufgekommen, um ein Buch zu holen, dessen ich bedurfte, und da wurde mir auf einmal unwohl — ich mag mich wohl ein wenig überanstrengt haben ... verzeihen Sie nochmals meine Störung und nehmen Sie meinen Dank für Ihre große Güte.“

Eine innere Stimme sagte ihm, daß es schicklich wäre, fortzugehen, allein er konnte ihr nicht augenblicklich gehorchen. Er sah vor sich auf die Erde und fühlte, daß die Augen des jungen Mädchens forschend auf ihm ruhten.

„Als ich Sie so blaß und verstört am Dachfirst stehen sah,“ sagte sie munter, „glaubte ich, daß Sie sich hinabstürzen wollten, und deshalb rief ich Sie so heftig an. Es hätte mir leid um Sie getan, denn Sie sind jung und das Leben ist so reich und schön! Finden Sie das nicht auch?“

Bent wurde verlegen, er hatte darüber noch niemals nachgedacht. Eigentlich kam es ihm vor, als wäre sein

Leben bisher weder besonders schön, noch vor allen Dingen reich gewesen, er wagte aber nicht zu widersprechen und stotterte nur:

„Ja, gewiß ... ganz wie Sie meinen."

Sie mochte ahnen, aus welchem Grunde Bent nicht so ganz einverstanden schien.

„Man kann mit wenigem zufrieden sein," entgegnete sie zuversichtlich, „und arm ist nur der zu nennen, der ein armes Herz hat. Dann gibt es ja auch so viel Herrliches, woran sich jeder freuen kann. Sehen Sie, jetzt kommt bald der Frühling — die Vögel werden singen, die Veilchen blühen und alles wird voll Fröhlichkeit und Sonne sein! O, Gott ist so gut und die Welt so unerfaßlich schön!"

Sie legte die Hand auf ihre Stirn und schwieg. Bent war sehr verwirrt, es fiel ihm ein, daß er noch nie in seinem Leben mit einem jungen Mädchen gesprochen habe. Er hätte gern etwas recht Kluges und Schönes gesagt, konnte aber nicht ein einziges Wort herausbringen. Er fühlte sich dumm und unglücklich, dennoch durchbebte sein Herz eine süße Bangigkeit, es war ihm sehr, sehr wunderbar zumute.

„Sie haben wohl nichts vom Frühling gewußt?" begann sie von neuem.

„Nein," sagte er zögernd, „ich hatte nicht Zeit dazu. Nun ist er aber gekommen und ich werde an ihn glauben, weil Sie ihn so liebhaben."

„Tun Sie das," entgegnete sie einfach, „und arbeiten Sie nicht zu viel. Gute Besserung."

Sie neigte leicht den Kopf und schritt die Stufen herab; über die Dächer fegte ein neuer Windstoß, er war merkwürdig warm, die Luft war trübe und regenschwer geworden. Das Mädchen verschwand durch die Tür, ohne sich einmal umzusehen; Bent konnte glücklicherweise seine schreckliche Verbeugung nicht mehr anbringen.

* * *

Bent ging langsam nach seinem Zimmer und vollendete seine Arbeit, dann sah er nach der Uhr und beschloß, nachmittags noch ins Kolleg zu gehen. Einstweilen warf er sich auf das Sofa, ein von Frau Bitterlich mit Stolz gehütetes Prokrustesbett, und versuchte seine Gedanken zu sammeln. Die Folge davon war, daß er in einen bleiernen Schlaf versank, der mehrere Stunden währte; als er erwachte, war es dunkel im Zimmer. Er sprang erschrocken auf, machte sich Vorwürfe über seine Zeitversäumnis und beschloß, da es zum Besuche der Kollegien zu spät, seine Arbeit wenigstens noch heute abzuliefern. Frau Bitterlich sah ihn verwundert an und wollte ihm, nachdem er seine übliche Meldung gemacht, das warmgestellte Mittagsbrot um jeden Preis einnötigen, er dankte jedoch und trat auf die Straße. Die Laternen waren eben angezündet worden, ein feiner Regen sprühte nieder, so unfühlbar, daß nur wenige der Vorübergehenden ihre Schirme aufgespannt hatten. Bent besann sich, daß sein Maschinenbauer am andern Ende der Stadt wohne, und schritt rüstig vorwärts, zuerst durch Straßen mit hell erleuchteten Läden, vor denen die Menschen standen, dann durch ein Viertel, wo die Laternen nur schwach brannten, wo die breiten Trottoirs holperigem, vor Nässe glänzendem Pflaster gewichen waren. Öde Bauplätze wechselten da mit eingezäunten, unfertigen Häusern, oder mit hohen, kasernenartigen Gebäuden. Hier und da ragte ein Schlot dunkel in die dunkle Nacht empor, das dumpfe, hastige Keuchen der Maschine tönte herüber; wenn das Tor aufging, fiel ein roter Flammenstreifen bis auf die andere Seite der Straße. Die war fast menschenleer, zuweilen nur kam ein rußiger Arbeiter, der seinem mühevollen Nachtdienste entgegenging, oder es rannte eine Frau vorüber, vielleicht verspäteter Einkäufe halber, vielleicht um Medizin für ein krankes Kind zu schaffen. Bent sah das gerne; ihm, dem Kinde der harten Arbeit, war dieses Treiben sympathisch. Hier war der Ort, wo es galt, das von der Wissenschaft Eroberte praktisch zu verwerten und der ganzen Menschheit dienstbar zu machen. Hier war ein System — hier war nur Fortschritt, kein Stillstand, kein Müßiggang; hier galt das Sprichwort: Selbst ist der Mann; hier hieß es arbeiten oder untergehen. Auch ich bin eine Nummer in der großen Zahl, dachte Bent — er gefiel sich in diesem Gedanken.

Der Maschinenbauer bewohnte ein abgelegenes Haus, welches von einem in der Entstehung begriffenen Garten umgeben wurde. Er war ein hervorragend tüchtiger Mann, der von unten herauf gedient hatte und sich seine Stellung selbst verdankte. Sein einziger Fehler bestand darin, daß er, als früherer Werkführer in einer großen

Fabrik, weder Gelegenheit, noch Zeit gefunden hatte, sich in höherer Mathematik fortzubilden, und nun, bei einzelnen schwierigen Fällen, von fremder Hilfe abhängig war. In dieser Angelegenheit ward ihm auf Befragen Bent als geeignete Persönlichkeit empfohlen. Bent hatte seitdem oft für ihn gearbeitet und sich seine Zufriedenheit in hohem Maße erworben. Der Maschinenbauer staunte über den hohen Grad von Auffassungsgabe, die Bent, selbst rein fachmäßigen Sachen gegenüber, bewies, ihm gefielen nicht minder die klaren Expositionen, die knappe Beweisführung; er nannte ihn scherzweise nur sein „technisches Bureau".

„Gut, daß Sie kommen", redete er ihn an, indem er ihm kräftig die Hand schüttelte. „Sind Sie mit unserer Berechnung fertig? Ja? Nun, das ist gut, jetzt wollen wir das Ding schon zustande bringen. Sie haben etwas auf sich warten lassen — war wohl kein leichtes Stück Arbeit, wie? Dachte mir's schon. Siemers und Gray haben vorgestern dasselbe Werk bekommen, es scheint aber auch damit zu hapern, denn heute beehrten mich die Herren vom Bureau und fragten, wie es mir denn eigentlich damit ginge? ‚Wird schon gehen', sagte ich. — Da standen sie denn eine Stunde um das Ding herum, wie die Ärzte an einem Krankenbett, und rechneten und machten lange Gesichter und empfahlen sich schließlich ... Aber kommen Sie doch herein, Sie müssen durchaus einen Löffel Suppe mit uns essen, meine Frau wird sich sehr freuen. He, Frau, wo steckst du? Ist das Abendbrot fertig?"

In diesem Augenblick öffnete sich die Tür und eine etwas kränklich aussehende Frau trat mit freundlichem Gruße ein. Ihr folgte eine Magd, welche die umfangreiche, dampfende Suppenschüssel trug; sie verschwand sogleich wieder und kehrte mit einem Brotlaib und einem mächtigen Steinkruge schäumenden Bieres zurück. Als der Tisch bestellt war, erhob sich ein etwa vierzehnjähriger Knabe von einem Reißbrett, über welchem er in einer Ecke des Zimmers gesessen hatte, und rief seinen Vater. Dieser besah die Zeichnung, einen ziemlich komplizierten Kegelschnitt, und nickte beifällig.

„Sehen Sie, Herr Sörensen," sagte er, „das bringt die Mittelklasse der Gewerbeschule doch noch nicht zuwege — na, es ist gut, mein Junge — leg deine Sachen ordentlich zusammen und komm zu Tische."

Das einfache Mahl wurde unter dem heiteren Geplauder der Kinder rasch verzehrt, dann wünschten sie den Eltern gute Nacht und reichten Bent die Hand, auch die Frau erhob sich und folgte den Kindern.

Der Maschinenbauer stopfte sich eine Pfeife und bot Bent eine Zigarre an.

„Ich danke," sagte dieser, „ich rauche nie."

Der Wirt lachte.

„Mit der können Sie es immerhin versuchen, sie ist nicht schwer. Oder rauchen Sie nicht aus Grundsatz?"

„Ich rauche sehr gern," entgegnete Bent, „tue es aber nie; erstens zieht es die Gedanken ab und zweitens ist es zum Leben nicht unbedingt notwendig."

Sein Gesicht hatte, während er so sprach, einen

strengen, beinahe alten Ausdruck bekommen. Der Maschinenbauer sah ihn von der Seite an und trommelte nachdenklich mit den Fingern auf dem Tische.

„Hm," meinte er nach einer kleinen Pause, „nichts für ungut, Herr Sörensen, aber was Sie da sagen, gefällt mir nicht. Man kann in sehr bescheidener Lage sein und doch ehrlich auskommen, ohne sich jeden kleinen Genuß versagen zu müssen. Ich spreche gar nicht vom Rauchen, aber ich bin überzeugt, daß Sie in Ihrem Leben noch niemals einen frischen, fröhlichen Spaziergang gemacht, oder einmal gute Musik oder ein Theaterstück gehört haben. Das stimmt nicht mit Ihrer Jugend und macht das Herz frühzeitig alt. Auch arbeiten Sie, glaube ich, zu viel; Sie sehen, nehmen Sie mir's nicht übel, recht eingetrocknet aus. Jedenfalls nehmen Sie es mit Ihrer Stellung viel zu ernst."

„Man kann nie zu viel arbeiten," entgegnete Bent kalt, „noch weniger kann ich es jemals mit meiner Stellung ernst genug nehmen. Ich bin der älteste Sohn einer armen, jedoch kinderreichen Predigerfamilie, mein Vater ist alt und ich daher sein natürlicher Vertreter. Jedes Zugeständnis, welches ich meinen eigenen Neigungen machte, jede Schwäche, die ich mir hingehen ließe, wäre Diebstahl an den Meinigen. Ich hoffe, daß Sie mir darin recht geben werden. Außerdem habe ich nur noch zwei Semester bis zum Staatsexamen und dann ist ja mein Ziel erreicht."

Der Maschinenbauer zog an seiner Pfeife, daß sie dichte Rauchwolken ausstieß.

„Es ist ja keine Frage," sagte er, „daß Sie das Examen bestehen werden wie kein zweiter, allein wie Sie dadurch einem bestimmten Ziele näher kommen, verstehe ich nicht. Haben Sie denn bereits irgend eine feste Aussicht?"

„Ja", sagte Bent widerstrebend. „Der Patron meines Vaters will sich unser erbarmen und hat mir nach bestandenem Examen eine Stelle als Vermesser zugesagt. Wenn ich die einmal habe, ist für die Meinigen gesorgt und die Not zu Ende. Nun wissen Sie alles."

Es lag große Bitterkeit in Bents Stimme. Er erhob sich und wollte gehen.

„Halt, nicht so, Herr Sörensen!" rief der Maschinenbauer, indem er seinerseits aufstand. „Ich sehe wohl, daß meine Neugier und die Lehre, welche ich Ihnen zu geben dachte, Sie verletzt haben, ich will aber kein ehrlicher Kerl sein, wenn ich es nicht gut mit Ihnen gemeint. Ich weiß, daß Sie arm sind und sich kümmerlich behelfen müssen, und deswegen hätte ich, wenn Sie mir nun eben nicht gesagt, daß bereits eine Stelle Ihrer warte, Ihnen vorgeschlagen, bis zum Examen bei uns zu wohnen, bei uns zu essen und nach der Prüfung ganz hier zu bleiben, um den technischen Teil meines Geschäftes zu übernehmen. Sehen Sie, das wollte ich nicht aus eigennütziger Absicht tun, sondern deswegen, weil ich Sie liebgewonnen habe und weiß, daß Sie ein ganzer Mann sind, trotz Ihrer großen Jugend. Wollte Gott, daß alle jungen Leute so wären wie Sie. Sehen Sie, das sagte ich mir, und sage es nun, da aus der Sache nichts mehr werden kann, erst recht. Wie ich aber über

Sie denke, wissen Sie jetzt — und von mir können Sie sich das ruhig gefallen lassen."

Er hatte sich ordentlich in Eifer geredet. Bent war durch sein treuherziges Anerbieten gerührt und dankte ihm mit warmen Worten, dann aber entschuldigte er sich, daß er aufbrechen müsse, es sei schon spät. Der Maschinenbauer begleitete ihn mit einem Lichte bis vor das Gartentor.

„Wir bleiben also gute Freunde!" rief er noch einmal.

„Solange Sie wollen", antwortete Bent. „Und glauben Sie, daß Ihre freundliche Anteilnahme mir das Herz warm gemacht hat."

Draußen regnete es nicht mehr, die Nacht war mild und dunkel, die Uhren schlugen tief und hell von allen Türmen. Bent eilte rasch nach Hause, seine Brust war voller Freude, das Lob des tüchtigen Mannes hatte ihm wohlgetan und ihn vor sich selbst erhöht. Es kam ihm vor, als sei heute der glücklichste Tag seines Lebens, als sei er plötzlich aus großer Dunkelheit erwacht ...

„Erwacht", sprach er mechanisch, „erwacht — und noch dazu kommt bald der Frühling." — Er blieb stehen und legte die Hand an die Stirn. Er sah sich auf den nassen Dächern, unter ihm waren Welt und Tod, vor ihm aber stand ein junges Mädchen, deren Haar im Frühlingssturm wehte und die zu ihm redete mit dunklen, errettenden Worten ...

Er neigte den Kopf und ging in Gedanken tief weiter.

„‚Gute Besserung' sagte sie mir," murmelte er leise, „gute Besserung, wie man's einem Kranken wünscht; ich glaube fast, sie hat recht, ich muß wohl krank gewesen sein, lange Jahre hindurch krank. Was sie damit wohl sagen wollte? Gleichviel, sie sagte ‚Gute Besserung' und ich glaube, ich bin schon ein besserer, glücklicherer Mensch geworden."

Dann stieg ihm ein Gedanke heiß zu Kopf. Wie war sein Benehmen so blöde und ungeschickt gewesen! Sie hatte ihm das Leben gerettet und er hatte sie nur angestarrt und ihr nicht einmal gedankt! Er preßte die Fäuste zusammen und stürmte vorwärts, als wolle er dem quälenden Gedanken entfliehen; die Empfindung, für lächerlich und undankbar gelten zu sollen, war ihm unerträglich. Er beschloß, einen langen Brief zu schreiben, oder baldmöglichst hinzugehen, um Verzeihung zu erbitten — was sollte sie aber trotzdem von ihm denken? Eine Weile noch rannte er in großer Aufregung weiter, dann hätte er fast einen Luftsprung getan. „Das wird's sein," sagte er befriedigt, „das ist es sogar." Er setzte heiter und still vor sich hinlächelnd seinen Weg fort. Bent Sörensen hatte offenbar einen guten Gedanken.

Indessen blieb das Fabrikviertel hinter ihm, die Laternen vermehrten sich und einzelne Wagen rasselten vorüber. In den Hauptstraßen waren noch viele Menschen, Bent freute sich, einmal zwecklos unter ihnen herumgehen zu können, auch blieb er vor jedem Laden stehen und sah neugierig in die lichtstrahlenden Schaufenster. Vor einem der letzteren sammelten sich die Vorübergehenden ganz besonders, es war größer und heller als die anderen und schien einem neuerrichteten

Geschäfte anzugehören. Sogar eine Equipage hielt davor, der Kutscher im weißen Regenmantel saß unbeweglich, die Peitsche in die Hüfte gestemmt, der Diener stand wartend am Wagenschlag. Unter die Schaulustigen gesellte sich auch Bent, er wollte die ausgestellten Dinge betrachten, welche sehr schön und lockend, fast nach einem gewissen System geordnet schienen. Da lagen herrliche Dinge, viele Früchte, die er nicht kannte und die ihn der symmetrischen Zusammenstellung halber besonders interessierten, ferner Terrinen mit langschnäbeligen Schnepfenköpfen darauf, dann mächtige, schwarzgrüne Vögel mit einer Schußwunde in der Brust, außerdem weiße Schachteln mit Silberdeckeln, Eingemachtes und Bonbons enthaltend. Bent wollte sich eben abwenden, als er in der obersten Reihe auch Blumen bemerkte, mattweiße Dinger in Spitzenpapier gehüllt, daneben aber einen frischen, blauen Veilchenstrauß. Er kehrte sofort um und blieb vor dem Fenster stehen, mit den acht Talern, die er soeben erhalten, verstohlen in der Tasche klimpernd. Das wäre sehr gut, dachte er — du bist ja gerade reich und außerdem hat sie etwas von Veilchen gesagt ...

Er trat entschlossen in den Laden. Es waren viele Menschen darin und er mußte ziemlich lange warten, ehe ihn eine korpulente, sehr geschäftig aussehende Frau anredete.

„Was beliebt, mein Herr?"

„Ich wünsche einen Veilchenstrauß zu kaufen", antwortete Bent, indem er sich bemühte, seiner Stimme einen möglichst nachlässigen Ausdruck zu geben.

„Hier, mein Herr — wollen Sie die Güte haben?“ Sie deutete auf ein hölzernes Regal, wo ein wahres Gebirge von Sträußen aufgespeichert lag.

Bent überflog die Situation mit forschendem Blick. Er nahm den kleinsten, den er entdecken konnte, und frug gleichgültig nach dem Preise.

„Anderthalb Taler, mein Herr, wenn's gefällig ist.“

Bent erschrak tödlich. Das war ja beinahe der vierte Teil seines Reichtums, und der war bereits so schön und sorglich eingeteilt! Zwei Taler für Kost, vier für die Wohnung, einer für Wäsche ...

Um sich einen Halt zu geben, prüfte er sorgfältig den feinen Duft der Blumen.

„Wie kommt es, daß die Veilchen so teuer sind?“ frug er endlich.

„Weil es noch nicht Frühling ist“, entgegnete die Verkäuferin ungeduldig, indem sie mit den Augen bereits an einer anderen Stelle des Ladens war, wo ein neuer Kunde ihrer harrte.

„So?“ sagte Bent verwundert. „Ich glaubte, es wäre schon Frühling.“

Ein junges Mädchen, das in Begleitung einer älteren Dame und eines ebenfalls bejahrten, aber gut konservierten Herrn am Verkaufstische stand, wandte sich hastig um.

Bent bezahlte seine Blumen und verließ den Laden. Draußen angelangt, stellte er sich noch auf einen Augenblick vors Schaufenster und überlegte, welches wohl der Preis der übrigen Dinge sein möge, wenn ein bescheidenes

Veilchenbukett allein eine so kolossale Summe koste; er wollte eben kopfschüttelnd gehen, als er ganz an der äußersten Grenze des Schaufensters ein kleines, notdürftig gekleidetes Mädchen bemerkte, welches, die Arme ins zerrissene Schürzchen gewickelt, fröstelnd dastand. Sie hatte sich dicht an die lichthellen Scheiben gedrückt, indessen große Tränen über ihr mageres Gesicht rannen.

Bent hatte bisher fremdes Elend selten beachtet, heute aber fühlte er sich sofort von Mitleid ergriffen und trat wie unabsichtlich an des Kindes Seite.

„Was fehlt dir, Kleine?" frug er sanft.

Das Kind hob den Kopf empor und sah ihn groß an. Ihre Augen blieben dabei auf dem Veilchenstrauß haften, als wollten sie sagen: Ja, du hast gut reden, du hast sogar Geld, um dir Blumen kaufen zu können . . .

Bent wurde verlegen, weil er fürchtete, daß die Dabeistehenden aufmerksam werden möchten; er beugte sich nieder und sagte fast zärtlich:

„Sprich doch, Kind, was fehlt dir?"

Die Kleine begann heftiger zu weinen.

„Mich hungert so", flüsterte sie endlich kaum hörbar.

Bent hielt das Geld, welches man ihm herausgegeben hatte, noch in der Hand; jetzt gab er es rasch dem Kinde und sagte:

„Da, nimm, und gib deiner Mutter auch etwas", dann versuchte er, sich davonzumachen.

Die Kleine hatte jedoch kaum das Silbergeld gesehen, als sie ihm nachlief und ihm durchaus die Hand küssen wollte. Bent konnte sich ihrer kaum erwehren, er wurde blutrot, weil mehrere der Vorübergehenden ihn teils mit erstaunten, teils mit beifälligen Blicken betrachteten.

Die Equipage mit den hohen braunen Pferden war unterdessen am Laden vorgefahren, der Diener reichte mehrere Pakete herein und blieb dann mit dem Hute in der Hand daneben stehen. Die Pferde scharrten ungeduldig auf dem Pflaster, wurden aber fest zurückgehalten. In dem geöffneten Schlage stand eine junge Dame und sah Bent unverwandt mit eigentümlichem Ausdruck an.

„Worauf wartest du, Giacinta?" rief eine Frauenstimme aus dem Wagen.

Die Tür war zugefallen, der Diener sprang auf den Bock und die Pferde stürmten in die Nacht hinaus. Bent sah beim Schein der Wagenlaternen ein blasses Gesicht mit großen dunklen Augen, das sich ihm hastig noch einmal zuwandte.

Er blieb stehen, wie vom Blitz getroffen, nur seine Lippen bewegten sich leise: Giacinta ... Giacinta ...

Bent ging am anderen Tage wie gewöhnlich ins Kolleg. Während der Frühstückspause erkundigte er sich bei einem Kommilitonen, welcher häufig ästhetische Tees besuchte und bei den Professorenfrauen Hahn im Korbe war, welche Zeit für die schicklichste gelte, um Visiten zu machen. Der Angeredete glaubte nicht recht gehört zu haben, sah Bent lachend von Kopf bis zu Fuß an und gab dann den gewünschten Bescheid: Elf bis eins für zeremonielle, drei bis fünf für zwanglosere Besuche. Unaufgefordert belehrte er Bent, daß diese den ersteren überhaupt, vornehmlich aber da vorzuziehen wären, wo es hübsche Töchter und guten Nachmittagskaffee gäbe. Sollte Bent aber gesonnen sein, dem Kultusminister eine Aufwartung zu machen, so müsse er ihm dringend raten, die Zeit von elf bis eins zu wählen, fernerhin Frack und weiße Krawatte anzulegen, das Ordensband über der Weste.

Bent dankte höflich, stand aber um punkt elf Uhr auf und verließ den Hörsaal. Zu Hause angekommen, holte er seinen schwarzen Rock hervor und betrachtete ihn nachdenklich; das gute alte Stück war ursprünglich für seinen Vater verfertigt worden, stand aber auch dem Sohne noch recht stattlich. Seine Toilette vervollkommnete er durch ein Paar Handschuhe, welche erst vor kurzem in voller Frische aus Frau Bitterlichs Wäsche gekommen waren, ergriff dann den Veilchenstrauß und begab sich klopfenden Herzens nach dem Nebenhause. Als er die schwere Tür aufstieß, erschien an einem zu ebener Erde angebrachten Fenster der höchst unordentlich frisierte Kopf eines Weibes, welches ihn mit Blicken musterte, wie man sie zuweilen bei Gendarmen bemerkt, wenn diese die Papiere eines verdächtigen Individuums prüfen. Das schon machte Bent verwirrt, er kam aber glücklich vorüber und ins erste Stockwerk. Es war zu vermieten, wie er aus einer daselbst befindlichen Anzeige ersah. Im zweiten Stock wohnte links ein Börsenagent, an der Entree rechts fehlte jede Andeutung, er faßte sich daher ein Herz und zog die Klingel. Ein Dienstmädchen, eine Tellerpyramide tragend, öffnete und frug nach seinem Begehr — er stand wie erstarrt. An dieses Hindernis hatte er noch gar nicht gedacht, er wußte ja nicht einmal, nach wem er fragen, bei wem er sich melden lassen sollte! Konnte er denn überhaupt eine junge Dame besuchen, ohne deren Angehörige zu kennen? Er wurde blutrot und stammelte Unzusammenhängendes, die Magd wiederholte ihre Frage und warf mit einem Schimpfworte die Türe zu. Es blieb nichts übrig, als den Rückzug anzutreten. Traurig schlich er die Treppen herunter, er kam sich unendlich beschämt und unglücklich vor. Nun war ja alles umsonst, der teure Veilchenstrauß sollte nutzlos verwelken, sein Dank unerhört bleiben — das schien ihm unerträglich hart. Er setzte sich hin und hatte gute Lust zu weinen; plötzlich sprang er auf, so heftig, daß der unglückliche, ohnedem schon morsche Stuhl krachend zu Boden fiel, und stürzte hinüber zu Frau Bitterlich.

„Ich bedarf noch eines Buches aus meiner Kiste," log er mit ziemlicher Gelassenheit. „Dürfte ich Sie noch einmal um den Bodenschlüssel bemühen?"

„Hier, Herr Sörensen," antwortete die Frau, indem sie sich eilfertig die ewig nassen Hände abtrocknete, „hier ist er. Warum kommen Sie denn eigentlich heute so früh aus dem Kolleg?"

„Weil ich Besseres zu tun habe", sagte Bent würdevoll, dann empfahl er sich ruhig wie immer; kaum draußen angelangt, stürmte er die Treppe hinauf. Beim Aufschließen des Bodens zitterten seine Hände derart, daß er sich gewaltsam zusammennehmen mußte; er atmete ein paarmal tief, trat an die Holztür und drückte hastig den Riegel — Gott sei Dank, sein Hoffen war erfüllt. Bei dem entstehenden Geräusch wandte Giacinta hastig den Kopf, ihre Brauen zogen sich unwillig zusammen, als sie aber Bent bemerkte, der mit seinem Strauße und dem glückseligsten Gesichte der Welt dastand, lächelte sie und schloß das Buch, darin sie geblättert. Bent war heute etwas sicherer, er trat auf das flache Dach hinüber, indem er im Kopfe noch rasch einmal die sorgsam einstudierten Worte überschlug, dann grüßte er und begann todesmutig:

„Gestatten Sie mir, mein Fräulein, mich nach Ihrem werten Befinden zu erkundigen und Ihnen nochmals meinen aufrichtigsten Dank für das Gute auszusprechen, welches Sie gestern an mir getan haben. Erlauben Sie ferner, daß ich Ihnen als Beweis meiner tiefgefühltesten Dankbarkeit einige von den Blumen überreiche, welche die Ehre haben, von Ihnen bevorzugt zu werden, und genehmigen Sie außerdem ..."

Sie unterbrach ihn durch eine barmherzige Bewegung. „Geben Sie," sagte sie einfach, „so — und nun hören Sie mich an. Ich nehme Ihre Blumen nicht, um Sie in dem Glauben zu bestärken, daß Sie irgendwie gegen mich verpflichtet seien — davon ist keine Rede. Ich nehme sie aber an, weil sie mich stets an eine gute Tat erinnern werden, deren Zeuge ich gestern war. Sie, mein Herr, hatten sich, um mir Freude zu machen, ein großes Opfer auferlegt, dennoch zögerten Sie keinen Augenblick, ein fremdes Elend zu lindern. Sie legten heimlich Ihre Gabe in die Hand des armen kleinen Kindes und flohen dann die Blicke der Leute — sehen Sie, das war gut, das war schön und darum nehme ich Ihre Blumen und danke Ihnen dafür von ganzem Herzen."

Ihre Stimme bebte, sie reichte Bent lebhaft die Hand — er fühlte einen leisen Druck der schlanken Finger, vor seine Augen kam es wie Nebel. „Giacinta," sprach er kaum hörbar vor sich hin — „Giacinta."

Ihre feinen Züge röteten sich unmerklich.

„Sie wissen also meinen Namen," sagte sie lächelnd, „nun gut, er ist ja auch kein Geheimnis. Aber nun noch eins. Bieten Sie mir nie wieder etwas an, begehen Sie nie wieder eine ähnliche Torheit für mich. Unter dieser Bedingung wollen wir gute Freunde bleiben. Haben Sie mich verstanden?"

Bent machte ein bekümmertes Gesicht.

„Sie sind so gut zu mir," stammelte er, „aber dies eine Mal erlauben Sie mir noch ... ich war noch nicht ganz fertig, es war noch nicht alles ..."

Er griff in die Brusttasche und brachte ein ziemlich umfangreiches Papierheft hervor.

„Bitte, nehmen Sie," sagte er schüchtern, „es macht mir so viel Freude!"

„O wie hübsch!" rief das junge Mädchen fröhlich, „es sind gewiß Gedichte, nicht wahr?"

„Gedichte? O nein", versetzte Bent gekränkt. „Dieses ist denn doch etwas Besseres, es hat einen nicht unerheblichen praktischen Wert ..."

Sie öffnete das Heft, sah natürlich nach der letzten

Seite und machte ein etwas verwundertes Gesicht. Auf dem Titelblatte stand: „Untersuchung über Hyperbeln höherer Art (Hyperboloiden). Seiner Lebensretterin in dankbarer Verehrung gewidmet von Bent Sörensen, Studiosus."

Sie sah ihn beinahe erschrocken an.

„Mein Gott, was ist das," sagte sie endlich, „was soll das heißen ... Hyper ... boloiden?"

Bent sammelte sich einen Augenblick und begann mit großer Genugtuung

„Hyperboloiden oder Hyperbeln höherer Art sind krumme Linien, worin die große Achse zum Parameter sich verhält wie das Produkt aus einer beliebigen Dignität der Summe der Zwergachse und Abszisse in eine beliebige Dignität der Abszisse zu der Semiordinate in der Dignität, deren Exponent der Summe jener anderen Exponenten gleich ist. Es gibt auch kubische, biquadratische, hyperbolische Hyperboloide ..."

Es war reizend von ihr, daß sie nicht hell auflachte, wozu sie die größte Lust hatte.

„Das ist gewiß wunderschön, Herr Bent Sörensen — nun weiß ich doch auch Ihren Namen — aber ich verstehe vorläufig kein Wort davon, Sie müssen mir es einmal bei Gelegenheit erklären. Einstweilen danke ich Ihnen sehr dafür. Nun will ich Ihnen aber etwas sagen: es ist nicht schicklich, daß wir zusammen auf den Dächern spazieren, die Nachbarn könnten darüber reden. Gehen Sie jetzt hübsch ruhig die Treppe hinunter und besuchen Sie uns heut' nachmittag auf dem landesüblichen Wege, ich werde einstweilen die Tante benachrichtigen. Wir wohnen im dritten Stockwerk."

Über Bents Antlitz flog ein Leuchten. Sie wohnte also nur eine Treppe tiefer als er, es lag keine zu unausfüllbare Kluft zwischen ihnen! Er hätte aufjubeln mögen vor Glück. Wie aber paßte der gestrige Abend dazu, an welchem ihm Giacinta vorbeigegangen war wie eine Erscheinung aus der Welt des Glanzes, die ihm so fremd war und die er so fürchtete?

Das junge Mädchen erriet seinen Ideengang.

„Wir sind nicht reich", sagte sie mit wehmütigem Lächeln. „Was den Wagen anbetraf, in dem Sie mich gestern sahen, so gehört er einer hiesigen angesehenen Persönlichkeit, an welche wir Empfehlungsbriefe hatten. Er ist ein Freund der Tante, glaub' ich," fügte sie mit seltsam zitternder Stimme hinzu, „und protegiert uns; Sie werden alles dieses später einmal genauer erfahren ... und nun noch eins. Meine gute Tante hat ein etwas eigentümliches Wesen, sie ist entsetzlich aufrichtig und pflegt zuweilen ihre geheimsten Gedanken recht deutlich auszusprechen. Wenn sie nicht ganz höflich zu Ihnen sein sollte, so nehmen Sie es ihr nicht übel, um meinetwillen, nicht wahr? Sie liebt mich ganz schrecklich," setzte sie mit trübem Lächeln hinzu, „und findet, daß eigentlich nur ein Prinz oder irgend ein anderes fabelhaftes Wesen meiner Bekanntschaft würdig wäre. So, nun wissen Sie, was Ihnen bevorsteht — wenn Sie Mut haben, so kommen Sie zu uns herüber, ich werde Sie erwarten."

Sie grüßte freundlich und wandte sich zum Gehen. Bent bemerkte, daß sie ihr Buch vergessen habe, er nahm es auf und gab es halb aufgeschlagen hin; dabei sah er, daß es Verse enthielt.

„Sie lieben Gedichte?" frug er ganz verwundert — ihm schien es aufzudämmern, daß er möglicherweise mit seiner Widmung der „Untersuchung über Hyperbeln höherer Art" zu verschwenderisch gewesen.

Das junge Mädchen lächelte.

„Ich liebe Gedichte so sehr," entgegnete sie, „daß ich mich auf das Dach verbanne, um mich ihrem Zauber ganz ungestört hingeben zu können. Ach, die deutschen Lieder sind so schön! Ich habe gehört, daß in Deutschland jeder junge Mann Gedichte schriebe — haben Sie es noch nie versucht?"

„Nein," versetzte Bent wegwerfend, „denn Gedichte haben nicht den geringsten Nutzen, es sind müßig ersonnene Reimereien, die durchweg jeder praktischen Bedeutung ermangeln."

Sie sah halb traurig auf ihn herab.

„Müßige Reimereien", sprach sie, „sind es nicht, denn ein fröhliches Herz fand noch niemals ein großes Lied. Alle Gedichte sind auch nicht ersonnen, die schönsten und besten wurden wohl immer erlebt. Poesie ist tiefer Schmerz, ist Liebe zu Gott, ihr fällt es zu, zur Menschheit zu reden, um sie größer und besser zu machen, was uns allen sehr not tut — und darum meine ich, daß man ihr Achtung schuldig ist, wenn man das Unglück hat, sie nicht lieben zu können."

Bent war durch die hübsche Art der Zurechtweisung sehr beschämt.

„Wenn Sie glauben, daß das Versemachen einen Nutzen hat," platzte er heraus, „will ich es auch einmal versuchen. Schwer kann es unmöglich sein, da es bereits so vielen gelungen ist."

Sie lächelte nur und neigte grüßend den Kopf. Bent ging wie traumbefangen auf sein Zimmer, schloß es ab und drückte die Stirn an die Scheiben. So stand er wohl eine Stunde; draußen war die Luft grau und der Regen rieselte nieder, die Leute sahen mit ihren Schirmen wie wandernde Pilze aus, auf den geschwollenen Gossen ließen Straßenkinder kleine Schiffe schwimmen. Er öffnete vorsichtig das Fenster, ein ganz warmer Luftstrom kam ihm entgegen. „Südwind", sprach er halblaut, dann stieß er die Flügel vollends auf, setzte sich an seinen Schreibtisch und beschloß, gleich heute ein schönes Gedicht anzufertigen. Als Form wählte er die Ode, weil Knappheit und Strenge doch einigermaßen zurechte dabei kamen, dann nahm er einen staubigen Horaz, den er in einer Ecke seines Büchergestells entdeckt hatte, und begann sich als Vorbild auszuschreiben:

„Integer vitae, scelerisque purus . . ."

„So," sagte er, „jetzt hätten wir die Formel, das ist die Hauptsache, der Rest wird sich schon finden." Er blieb einige Minuten über das Papier gebeugt, dann erhob er den Kopf mit einer unendlich erstaunten Miene, er hatte die wichtige Entdeckung gemacht, daß die Form an und für sich, ohne irgend einen kleinen Gedanken, eigentlich nichts sei. Bestürzt las er das Gedicht noch einmal durch und verweilte besonders nachdenklich bei der letzten Strophe:

„Pone sub curru nimium propinqui
Solis in terra domibus negata:
Dulce ridentem Lalagen amabo,
Dnlce loquentem —"

Das einzige, was er fand, war, daß Lalage lange nicht so hübsch laute wie Giacinta. Er begann darauf das Papier mit einer großen Anzahl kunstreich verschlungener G zu bedecken, dann hielt er plötzlich inne. „Mit der Ode", sprach er vor sich hin, „ist es nichts, die Form ist auch vielleicht zu altmodisch, ich muß ein Metrum nehmen, welches mir vertrauter ist, welches mehr Fall hat." Er überschlug im Geiste die Gedichte, die er in seiner Kinderzeit hatte lernen müssen, fand aber lange nichts Passendes. Endlich belebten sich seine Züge, er nahm hastig die Feder und schrieb:

„Lenore fuhr ums Morgenrot
Empor aus schweren Träumen"

„Das ist's," rief er halblaut, „darin liegt eine schöne Regelmäßigkeit, fast eine gewisse Kongruenz der Strophen."... Er begann sein Hirn mit frischem Mute zu zermartern, trotz der gepriesenen Kongruenz war es ihm jedoch nicht möglich, eine vernünftige Zeile, einen einzigen armen Reim zusammenzuhaspeln. Allmählich schien der Gedanke in ihm aufzudämmern, daß es mit der Dichtkunst einen besondern Haken haben müsse. Er stützte den Kopf in die Hand und verfiel in tiefes Nachdenken, ein paar Worte kamen ihm in den Sinn, die Giacinta gesprochen: ein fröhliches Herz fand niemals ein großes Lied. „Das ist es," rief er aufspringend, „ich kann nicht dichten, weil mein Herz zu voll, zu glücklich ist, weil ich dich wiedersehen soll, Giacinta, heute noch, jetzt gleich ..."

Ein heftiger Windstoß kam durchs offene Fenster, in den Gassen begann es dunkel zu werden. Er blickte noch einige Minuten in die Dämmerung, dann begab er sich langsam nach dem Nebenhause. Im zweiten Stocke traf er das Dienstmädchen, welches ihn so hart angelassen hatte, sie kauerte am Boden und wusch mit feuerroten Armen die Treppe.

„Entschuldigen Sie, daß ich Sie vorhin unnütz bemüht," sagte Bent sanft, „ich hatte mich in der Etage geirrt."

Das Mädchen, dem man wohl selten freundlich war, betrachtete ihn verwundert. Er überschritt vorsichtig die nassen Stufen und kam an eine hohe Glastür; auf einer Visitenkarte, die unter dem Glockenzuge angebracht war, stand: Signora Galieri, Vicolo Giuliano 55.

Als er die Klingel zog, antwortete das gellende Gekläff eines kleinen Hundes, dann öffnete Giacinta rasch die Tür und bat ihn einzutreten.

„Ich habe die Tante auf Ihren Besuch vorbereitet," sagte sie, „meine liebe Zia ist heute sehr guter Laune." Diese Worte sprach sie ziemlich laut, und den Kopf nach dem Zimmer gewendet: „Nun folgen Sie mir."

Sie öffnete die Tür eines einfachen kleinen Eßsaals,

schlug einen Vorhang zurück und führte den Besucher in einen merkwürdig großen Raum, darin halbe Dämmerung herrschte. In der entlegensten Ecke des Zimmers befand sich eine Hängematte, sie umschloß eine höchst stattliche, hochfrisierte Dame von etwa vierzig Jahren, neben dieser stand ein Tischchen mit Nippsachen und einem Teller voll Orangen, darüber wiegte sich in seinem vergoldeten Ringe ein schöner, buntgefiederter Papagei.

Die Dame richtete sich auf.

„Hier, Zia," sagte das junge Mädchen fröhlich, „bringe ich dir Herrn ... Herrn ... Bent fängt sein Name an, so viel habe ich mir glücklich behalten. Er will dir seine Aufwartung machen und ich finde es sehr hübsch von ihm, daß er trotz des schrecklichen Wetters zu uns gekommen ist."

Bent hatte während dieser einführenden Worte Gelegenheit gefunden, zweimal seine Verbeugung anzubringen, und stand jetzt unter dem Blicke, den er auf sich geheftet fühlte, etwas verlegen da.

Die Zia hatte bald ihr Examen beendet.

„Ma che!" sagte sie zu Giacinta achselzuckend und mit unendlich mitleidiger Stimme, „che poveretto!"

Sie legte sich ungeniert in ihre Matte zurück und begann, indem sie Deutsch und Italienisch auf das erbarmungsloseste durcheinander mischte, eine Unterhaltung über das schlechte Wetter, über den trostlosen Aufenthalt im Norden überhaupt, wo man die Sonne gar nicht sähe und die Leute so wenig gentilezza besäßen.

Dieses Thema schien der würdigen Dame sehr geläufig zu sein; um die von ihr angeführten zahlreichen Schattenseiten noch kräftiger hervorzuheben, begann sie plötzlich von Italia bella zu sprechen. Ihre Augen leuchteten, die deutschen Worte wurden immer seltener, endlich flossen ganze Sätze in der Toskanersprache dahin. Giacinta hatte eine Arbeit zur Hand genommen und Bent saß lauschend da, zuweilen hob er die Augen auf und sah vor sich das süße Köpfchen mit den dunklen Brauen und dem sinnigen, feinen Profil, in seinem Ohre schwammen weiche, unverständliche Laute, dazwischen kamen zuweilen deutsche Worte in seltsamer Betonung, blühendes Land, blaues Wasser, Sonnenschein, Glück und ewige Jugend. Es war ganz dunkel und still im Zimmer, nur an die Scheiben rauschte der Frühlingsregen ...

Madame Galieri brach plötzlich ab.

„Davon verstehen Sie ja doch nichts", sagte sie verächtlich. Sie warf sich auf die andere Seite, schälte eine Orange und steckte Bent ohne weiteres ein Stück in den Mund; dann seufzte sie ein paarmal, klagte, daß in Deutschland alles langweilig sei, und verlangte endlich ein Spiel Karten, um Patience zu legen. Giacinta sprang schnell auf, zündete ein Licht an, das auf einem kleinen Tische harrte, und rückte dann näher zu Bent.

„Kommen Sie," sagte sie lächelnd, „nun können auch wir einmal plaudern; die Zia ist fürs erste ganz in ihre Karten, die ihr niemals nach Wunsch einschlagen, versenkt. Vor allen Dingen müssen Sie mir jetzt von Ihrer Jugend erzählen, von Ihrem Vaterhause und Ihrer nordischen Heimat; ich höre so gern", fügte sie wehmütig scherzend hinzu, „von Kinderglück und Heimat reden."

Bent gehorchte. Er sprach von Jütland, dem stillen, melancholischen Lande mit seinen Buchenwäldern und kühlen blauen Fjorden, seinen endlosen Heiden, über denen im Frühjahr die Lerche singt und im Herbst die Sommerfäden ziehen, dann von den Hünengräbern, auf denen oft eine einsame Buche steht, die knorrigen Äste trotzig niederzwingend auf den Hügel, von den Mooren, die kein Fuß je betrat, und die so schwarz und todstill liegen, daß man sich fürchten möchte, über denen kein Laut ist, als das Schwirren des Kiebitzes oder des Regenpfeifers klagender Schrei. Er erzählte von den dämmerigen, kurzen Tagen, den endlosen Winternächten, von den Novemberstürmen, die durch das Land brausen und den Schnee berghoch zusammentreiben, daß Wege und Dörfer verweht und die Bewohner oft wochenlang von menschlichem Verkehr abgeschnitten sind ... sie lieben ihr Vaterland um so fester, diese schwerfälligen, schweigsamen Jüten mit den flachsblonden Köpfen und den riesigen, von Arbeit verbogenen Gliedmaßen, sie lieben es mit einer Art finsterer Treue, sie treiben hin ein Leben ohne Abwechslung, ohne Klang und ohne Freude, eingespannt in den Schraubstock stumpfer Pflichterfüllung, den Nacken krumm vor Gott und dem Amtmanne. So war es auch auf dem armen Pfarrdorfe an der Westküste, die Jahre flossen dahin in Einsamkeit und streng geregeltem Tagewerke, da war keine Anregung, keine geistige Erholung; die einzigen Bücher, welche die Kinder in den seltenen Mußestunden lesen durften, bestanden aus ein paar Erbauungsschriften und dem Staatskalender. Es war kein freundliches Bild, welches Bent malte — nirgends war eine lichte Jugenderinnerung, ein Anklang von Glück, überall nur Einförmigkeit, Härte, rastlose Arbeit. Und selbst die Natur hatte keine mildernde Wirkung ausüben können, sie war karg und streng wie alles dort oben.

„Ich habe einmal", sagte Bent, „von einem Pastorate in Deutschland gehört, welches ganz von Linden umgeben sein soll. Das muß wunderschön sein, wir haben nie eine Linde gehabt."

Er erzählte weiter, mit so ruhiger Stimme, als ob er mit allem einverstanden wäre, dennoch lag in seinen Worten ganz unabsichtlich Entsagung und tiefe Resignation. Seine Geschichte verlief auch bald im Sande, er wußte nichts weiter zu sagen und sah schüchtern zu Giacinta auf, ob er sie auch nicht gelangweilt habe. Das schien aber nicht der Fall gewesen zu sein, sie hatte den Kopf auf ihre gefalteten Hände gelegt und sah ihn nachdenklich an; die Signora wendete zuweilen mit einem halblauten Ausrufe ihre Karten, und der Papagei wiegte sich schlaftrunken in seinem Ringe.

„Ihr Leben war nicht froh," sagte sie endlich, „das meine noch weniger. Ich habe meine Mutter nie gekannt; mein Vater war ein hoher Offizier und fiel für seinen König. Ich hatte niemand auf der Welt als die Zia, welche einst eine sehr berühmte Sängerin war. Sie nahm sich meiner an, und nun werde auch ich bald singen, um meinen Lebensunterhalt zu erwerben."

Sie hatte die Worte müde und gleichgültig hingeworfen, als spräche sie von einer Fremden, Bent aber fühlte sich aufs tiefste ergriffen. Er hatte doch noch Eltern, Geschwister, eine Heimat — wie war er reich diesem verlassenen fremden Kinde gegenüber! Er mußte wohl arbeiten, aber das war ja auch ganz in der Ordnung, er konnte es. Sie jedoch sollte von Ort zu Ort ziehen, für Geld singend, von tausend Augen begafft und bemäkelt? Er war noch niemals in einem Theater oder Konzerte gewesen, er erinnerte sich aber an das Bild einer Sängerin, welches er einmal vor Jahren irgendwo gesehen: sie hatte ein Pantherfell über dem entblößten Busen und ein Weinglas in der Hand ... sollte dieses stille, blumenhafte Wesen einst werden wie jene? Nimmermehr! Er fühlte ein körperliches Weh im Herzen, er begann zu sprechen, unzusammenhängend, ungeschickt, aber ein Sturm von Leid und Leidenschaft war es, der aus seinen Worten brach. Das junge Mädchen saß ihm still gegenüber, ihre Augen standen voll Tränen. Über sein eigenes Schicksal, sein eigenes armes, verkümmertes Leben hatte er nicht geklagt, fremdes Leid aber machte sein Herz erbeben, trieb ihm Flammen auf die Stirn, grollende Worte auf die Lippen — o, er war gut! Sie mußte der Gabe gedenken, die er dem Bettelkinde gegeben. Das war nur eine flüchtige Regung des Mitleids, wieviel größer und zarter war die Wohltat, die er jetzt ihr durch seine herzliche, warme Teilnahme erwies. Er tröstete sie, so gut er konnte, der arme Junge mit dem schlechtsitzenden Rocke und der vor Erregung zitternden Stimme; er ahnte es wohl nicht, mit wie heißer Dankbarkeit sich das verwaiste und doch so volle Herzchen ihm zuwandte, er ahnte es nicht, denn er schwieg verlegen und marterte seinen Hut, den er bis jetzt krampfhaft in der Hand behalten.

„Cara mia, amüsierst du dich gut?" rief die Signora hinüber, indem sie eine neue Kartenreihe auflegte.

Giacinta machte eine Bewegung, als ob sie erwache.

„Ich danke, Zia", antwortete sie kühl; dann wandte sie sich zu Bent. „Bedauern Sie mich nicht zu sehr," sagte sie, „denn ich singe gern, aus voller Seele gern ... wenn Sie es wollen, will ich Ihnen gleich etwas singen und das, so gut ich's immer kann."

Ihre Stimme war wunderweich, dennoch zuckte es herb um ihren Mund, als ob sie mit Tränen kämpfe. Sie erhob sich und trat einen Schritt vorwärts.

„Ma Giacinta, che idea!" rief die Tante erstaunt und besorgt, „du hast heute schon viel zu lange geübt, du wirst dich mit Gewalt krank machen! Wenn dich der Hofrat einmal um eine Arie bittet, bist du regelmäßig müde, heiser oder weiß der Himmel was noch, jetzt dagegen willst du auf einmal für nichts und wieder nichts singen. Dio mio, welche Laune!"

„Laß mich, Zia", erwiderte das junge Mädchen ruhig. „Ich bin eben jetzt in der rechten Stimmung und werde mich nicht ermüden."

Sie ging nach einem Teil des Zimmers, der ganz

im Dunkeln lag, und entzündete die Kerzen auf zwei fünfarmigen Leuchtern. Ein festliches Licht drang durchs Gemach, dieses war aber so groß, daß nur ein schöner altmodischer Flügel und ein Teil der Wand hell übergossen war, daran hingen silberne und goldene Blumenkronen mit langen Atlasbändern, auf denen Widmungen, an Signora Galieri oder an die Diva Galieri gerichtet, zu lesen waren. Der Rest des Zimmers lag in halber Dämmerung, nur blitzte zuweilen eine Goldleiste hervor oder der Rahmen eines Bildes. Dann strömte eine Flut von Akkorden durch den Raum und plötzlich erwachte daraus eine weiche, wunderbar süße Stimme:

„O primavera, gioventù di' vita . . .“

Die Zia hatte gleich bei den ersten Klängen ihre Karten weggeworfen und sich hastig aufgerichtet. Es war, als sei neues Leben in sie gekommen, sie nickte beständig mit dem Kopfe oder fuhr mit den Armen in der Luft umher, dann sah sie Bent triumphierend, mit blitzenden Augen an. Endlich konnte sie sich nicht mehr bezwingen: fast ehe der letzte Ton verhallt war, umhalste sie das junge Mädchen und bedeckte sie mit leidenschaftlichen Liebkosungen.

„Angelo mio, ti farai male ... benedetta ragazza, t'amo tanto ... und Ihr, Signore, was sagt Ihr dazu? So etwas hört man nicht in Eurem Bärenlande! Ah, Giacinta, sieh — der poveretto ist ganz bestürzt ... ah, tu sei un' incantatrice ...“

Giacinta hatte den Sturm von Worten und Zärtlichkeiten still über sich ergehen lassen; als Bent herantrat, hob sie zum erstenmal das Auge von den Tasten; sie lächelte schwach, wie er so vor ihr stand und mit heißen Wangen und ganz abwesenden Augen nach Worten rang. Sie sah ihm ins Herz und fühlte, was er sagen wollte: Ich stehe auf einem Felsen und sehe vor mir eine lichte, nie gekannte Welt, ich sehe hinein mit fremden Augen, die sich dem Frühlinge öffnen möchten, aber der Sturm umbraust mich, mich faßt ein Schwindel — dann sehe ich wieder allein nur dich und mir ist es, als müßte ich knien vor dir, als seiest du selber der Frühling ...

Er hatte auch wirklich etwas ähnliches gestammelt, dann war es ihm, als müsse er fortgehen, fortgehen, um allein zu sein. Er suchte nach seinem Hute und empfahl sich; die Signora sagte ein paar unverständliche Worte, Giacinta gar nichts. So lief er hinaus in den Regen.

Und es regnete die ganze Nacht durch, unablässig, wie es nur an Winters Ende regnen kann, es troff von den Dächern, es strömte in den Gossen, graue Wolken zogen so niedrig über die Stadt, daß sie fast die Giebel der Häuser streiften. Bent saß im Kolleg und sah den Tropfen zu, welche über die Scheiben rieselten, es war so dunkel im Hörsaal, daß man kaum nachschreiben konnte. Niemand hatte rechte Lust zum Arbeiten, auch der Vortrag des Professors war monoton, gleichsam in Grau gehalten; endlich schlug es 5 Uhr und Bent wanderte durch die triefenden Gassen nach Hause. Auf der Treppe empfing ihn Frau Bitterlich mit der Nachricht, daß seit einer Stunde Besuch auf ihn warte; es sei ein

Herr, namens von Versen, ein sehr feiner und liebenswürdiger junger Mann. Er habe sich zwei Lichter anzünden lassen, eine Zigarre zu rauchen begonnen und mit ihrem Manne, welcher gerade die Gardinen erneuert, sehr freundlich geplaudert. Bent stieg etwas verwundert die Treppe hinauf — von Versen war der Name jenes jungen Dichters, jenes Mitgliedes der Tafelrunde, vor welchem er sich fürchtete — dann betrat er unruhvoll sein Zimmer. Er hatte sich nicht getäuscht, George von Versen war es, der von dem harten Sofa aufsprang und ihm lachend die Hand bot.

„Gestehen Sie, daß Sie eher erwartet hätten, den Rattenfänger von Hameln in Ihrem Zimmer vorzufinden, als meine Wenigkeit," rief er lustig, „die Sache verhält sich aber einfach. Sie ließen sich viele Abende bei uns nicht blicken, und da wir alle Ihre Regelmäßigkeit und Gewohnheitsliebe kennen, sind wir auf den Gedanken gekommen, daß Sie uns etwas übelgenommen haben müßten. Es ist mir nun eingefallen, daß ich möglicherweise der Stein des Anstoßes sein könne, indem ich neulich, freilich auf den Wunsch der übrigen Herren, meine ‚Wanderlieder' vorgetragen habe. Die Herren, welche Ihre Abneigung gegen alles, was Gedicht heißt, kennen, wollten Sie natürlicherweise etwas zum besten haben, und ich bin vielleicht zu bereitwillig auf ihre Intentionen eingegangen. Da Sie seit jenem Abende fortgeblieben sind und ich nicht will, daß Sie einer Neckerei wegen Ihres einzigen Vergnügens beraubt werden, bin ich zu Ihnen gekommen, um offen mit Ihnen zu reden. Wenn ich mich nur irgendwie im Unrecht glaube, halte ich niemals mit einer Entschuldigung zurück — ich liebe es nicht, auf meinem Wege Unklarheiten und Mißhelligkeiten zu begegnen. Das war es, was ich Ihnen sagen wollte, lieber Sörensen, und es bleibt mir nur noch hinzuzufügen, daß wohl jeder einzelne in unserem kleinen Kreise so über die Sache denkt, wie ich es tue, und daß es unter der ganzen Tafelrunde gewiß keinen gibt, der Ihnen nicht die Zuneigung und Achtung entgegentrüge, die Ihnen reich gebührt."

Er hatte mit so viel Sicherheit und so viel richtigem Gefühl gesprochen, daß Bent ganz gerührt wurde. Die ihm dargebotene Hand drückend, gelobte er, daß er nie daran gedacht habe, den Empfindlichen zu spielen; sein Nichterscheinen habe einen andern Grund, er sei überhaupt in letzter Zeit etwas aus seiner gerühmten Regelmäßigkeit herausgekommen. Jedenfalls wolle er heute abend das Versäumte nachholen und bei der Tafelrunde erscheinen, worauf er sich sehr freue.

Versen ließ ihm kaum Zeit zum Ausreden.

„Ja," rief er lachend, „auch Ihre Wirtin hat mir bereits geklagt, daß Ihr Lebenswandel seit einiger Zeit an bedeutenden Schwankungen leide! Früher wären Sie pünktlich zehn Minuten nach fünf heimgekommen und um sieben wieder fortgegangen — mit der schönen Regelmäßigkeit habe es jetzt jedoch ein Ende. Anstatt um fünf kämen Sie manchmal schon um drei und gingen dann aus, um erst zu nächtlich später Stunde heimzukehren — an ein Adieusagen, wie Sie es doch früher stets getan hatten, wäre gar nicht mehr zu denken. Die biedere Frau beendigte ihre Rede damit, daß sie für heute Ihr Nachhausekommen überhaupt als äußerst fragwürdig darstellte, mir aber schließlich doch noch den Rat erteilte, in Ihrem Zimmer zu warten. Dazu war ich allerdings von vornherein entschlossen, weil ich nicht unverrichteter Sache heimziehen wollte.

„Ich richtete mich also häuslich bei Ihnen ein, steckte eine Zigarre an und hatte ein äußerst lehrreiches Gespräch mit Ihrem Hauswirte, welcher mir verschiedener wirtschaftlicher Obliegenheiten halber Gesellschaft leistete. Als er fortgegangen war, als ich Ihr Zimmer genugsam eingeräuchert hatte, begann ich mich erschrecklich zu langweilen und unterzog demzufolge Ihre Bibliothek einer Besichtigung. Das erste Buch, welches ich ergriff, enthielt nichts als Formeln, ich ließ es daher entsetzt fallen. Die anderen Bücher waren ähnlichen Schlages, da endlich ward mir Ihr Schreibtisch zum Quell in der Wüste, denn auf ihm lag mein geliebter Horaz, in den ich mich sofort vertiefte. Ich habe ihn zwar noch nie vergebens vorgenommen und noch nie ohne Nutzen aus der Hand gelegt, aber daß mir der alte Bursche zu einer so kostbaren Entdeckung verhelfen würde, hätte ich nimmermehr geglaubt! Ich habe herzlichst lachen müssen und spüre jetzt gute Lust, wieder von vorn anzufangen. Verzeihen Sie, Bent, es war aber wirklich zu komisch."

„Was denn," frug Bent erstaunt, „was haben Sie entdeckt?"

„Denken Sie sich, als ich an das integer vitae komme, finde ich einen Briefbogen mit Versen nach dem Metrum der Ode, aber leider durchgestrichen und ganz unleserlich. Dagegen war jedoch das Wort Lalage wohl fünfzigmal hingemalt und daneben stand: Lenore fuhr ums Morgenrot. Es ist wirklich köstlich! Ich komme zu Ihnen, um Abbitte zu leisten, weil ich Ihr Ohr mit meinen Versen verletzt zu haben wähnte, und muß schon in der ersten Viertelstunde in Ihnen den Kollegen in Apoll begrüßen. Bent, Bent, Sie sind ein großer Tartüff!"

Bent war entsetzt aufgesprungen und hatte das Blatt ergriffen. Gott sei Dank, da stand nichts Verräterisches, nur hatte seine Hand ein paarmal angesetzt: Gia — Gia — war aber nicht weiter gekommen. Gia war kein Name, es war also noch einmal gnädig abgegangen. Er wandte sich wieder um und versuchte sogar zu lächeln, der Schreck saß ihm aber noch dergestalt in den Gliedern, daß er bald blaß, bald rot wurde.

Versen saß ihm gegenüber und lachte noch immer.

„Haben Sie es übelgenommen, daß ich hinter Ihr Geheimnis geraten bin?" sagte er, plötzlich ernster werdend. „Glauben Sie mir, ich freue mich herzlich, daß wir auch darin Geistesgenossen sind, und niemand, ich verspreche es Ihnen, soll von meiner Entdeckung erfahren. Weiß ich es doch selber am besten, daß die heilige Blume gern im geheimen emporsprießt. Erst wenn sie sich entfaltet hat, darf sie sich dem Winde bieten; erst wenn sie duftet, darf sie für die Menschheit blühen. Ich weiß das sehr wohl, Bent, und Sie dürfen sich mir dreist erschließen. Wollen Sie mir vertrauen, wollen wir von heute ab gemeinschaftlich dichten, gemeinschaftlich arbeiten?"

„Sie irren sich", sagte Bent traurig. „Ich bin kein Dichter, ich war nie anders, als ich mich gezeigt habe. Ihr alle kennt ja mein Leben und meine Aussichten — wie könnten aus solchem Boden wohl Gras und Blumen kommen? Freilich, seit einiger Zeit ist ein Kampf in mir, ein Teil meiner Seele will sich heben, will frei sein, will fliegen, Gott weiß wohin — ein anderer aber drückt das alles wieder bleiern nieder. Es ringt und wogt in mir, es ist fast, als ob junges, brausendes Wasser mit dem Eise kämpfte, das darauf liegt, und es brechen wollte. Sie kennen das vielleicht selber oder verstehen mich wenigstens, wenn es nicht zu großer Unsinn ist, den ich da geredet habe ..."

„Nein, Bent," rief Versen aufspringend, „Unsinn ist das nicht, bei Gott, das ist es nicht. Ich kenne jenes Gefühl, es kommt im Leben nur einmal. Und was das bedeutet, weiß ich auch — es kündet eine Umwälzung an, einen Sturm, der alles brechen wird, was morsch in deiner Seele. Es ist eine Katastrophe, es geht dabei um Leben oder Tod. Höre, Bent — sei mein Freund. Gib mir die Hand, lieber Junge — so — zweie tragen besser als einer. Deine arme, verkümmerte Jugend bricht hinter dir zusammen, du kannst es nicht ändern. Was aus dir werden wird, weiß Gott allein — jedenfalls war es sein Hauch, der deine Stirn gestreift. Sei jener Sturm, der in dir wach wird, der des Genies, sei es der einer großen Leidenschaft — folge ihm ohne Kampf, gib dich ihm hin ohne Trotz. Möglich ist's, daß du glücklich, wahrscheinlich, daß du unglücklich wirst — frage nicht danach, sondern denk daran, daß Sonnenkuß und Blitzschlag beide von Gott kommen. Du wirst ein Mensch werden, der anders als die meisten, du wirst einsam stehen, das Herz voll Sturm, voll Gedanken, voller Liebe — dann, Bent, dann schweige nicht, dann verschließe dich nicht, du littest sonst nutzlos. Alles, was du hast, deinen Groll, deine Kraft, deine Liebe, gib es hin an die Menschheit, sie bedarf dessen. Dich selbst wird man den Ritter der Mancha nennen — gleichviel, senke die Lanze und reite hinein in die Windmühlenflügel, hinein in die Hammelherde der Dummheit. Man wird dich schmähen — schüttle Spott und Hohn ab wie Regentropfen. Bleibe treu und unentwegt, wolle das Große und tue rastlos das Gute; dann wird dein Leben zwar kurz sein und ein einziger Kampf, reich nur an Täuschung und Schmerz, auf dein Grab aber werden einst die Sonnen scheinen, deren Glanz du prophetisch geahnt, und über den vergessenen Hügel wird der große Wanderzug der Menschheit gehen, dem fernen Ziele, der endlichen Vollkommenheit, dem Morgen zu."

Seine Lippen bebten und seine Augen sprühten. Bent bot ihm beide Hände und legte den Kopf auf seine Schulter.

„Nimm mich hin," sagte er, „du mein erster und einziger Freund."

Das währte eine Minute, dann machte sich Versen sanft frei.

„Es ist spät geworden," sagte er lustig, „begleite mich nach Hause, Bent. Es ließe sich da vielleicht eine Flasche Rheinwein auftreiben, um das Wohl unserer jungen Freundschaft zu trinken."

Sie gingen Arm in Arm durch die Straßen, die Laternen brannten dunstig im Nebel, ihr Schein irrte über schwarze Wasserlachen und halb geschmolzene Schneemassen. Nach einer Zeit blieb Bent stehen.

„Höre, George," sagte er mit schüchterner Stimme, „du hast vorhin Worte gesprochen, die mich sehr ergriffen haben. Du hast recht, es ist eine Umwälzung in mir, die mich beseligt und vor der mir's zugleich graut. Es ist kein himmelstürmender Geist, der in mir durchbricht — ich habe gar kein Genie. Also muß es", er stockte und das Blut schoß ihm ins Gesicht, „etwas ... etwas... vielleicht das andere sein, wovon du geredet hast. Verzeihe mir, ich bin so ganz unwissend und ohne Halt, es hat sich noch niemand außer dir um mich bekümmert ... ich habe noch mit keinem so etwas gesprochen: warum liebt man ein junges Mädchen so ... so ... ganz merkwürdig anders, als man Eltern oder Geschwister liebt? Frauenliebe muß also die höchste Liebe sein ... was ist eigentlich diese Liebe, George? Du bist viel erfahrener als ich, du bist sogar, wie man sagt, ein Dichter ... du mußt es also ja ganz genau wissen."

Versens Lippen hatten sich zu einem halben Lächeln gezogen, er wurde aber sogleich wieder ernst.

„Deine Frage, lieber Bent, verdient eine andere Antwort, als ich dir zu geben vermag. Die Weisheit hört an diesem Punkte leider auf, kein Dichter und kein Denker hat jemals eine erschöpfende Definition gefunden. Chamfort und der Apostel Johannes sind darüber ganz verschiedener Ansicht. Die Liebe ist der Ariadnefaden, der uns durch ein sehr dunkles Labyrinth leiten soll; leider ward er für die meisten Menschen zu kurz gesponnen. Liebe ist die Verwandtschaft mit Gott, sie ist die einzige menschliche Eigenschaft, die nicht klein sein kann. Es gibt keine kleinliche Liebe. Liebe ist vielleicht Abglanz aus einer verlorenen, besseren Welt, der uns im Herzen geblieben ist. Liebe ist Anfang und Ende, Menschenwitz kann sie nicht ermessen. Frage keinen Weisen, keinen Philosophen, was Liebe ist — frage die Frau, die du liebst, und Gott darum."

„Und du selbst," sagte Bent nach langem inneren Kampfe, „du selbst, George, liebst du?"

„Wir sind seit einer Stunde Freunde," sagte Versen rauh, „dafür klingt deine Frage seltsam. Mir ist es aber, als müßte ich dir vertrauen, als wäre es unrecht, wenn ich's nicht täte. Ich hatte nie geliebt — seltsam genug in unserer frühreifen Zeit — jetzt tu' ich's seit kurzen Tagen, es ist über mich gekommen wie ein Schlag, wie eine Offenbarung, in mein Traumleben hinein wie eine Erlösung. Du sagst, meine Liebe müsse echt sein? O ja. — Du meinst, sie würde glücklich werden? O nein, tausendmal nein. Sieh Bent, die Frau, die meinem Leben so frühe Sonnenwende gebracht — ich habe sie nur einmal gesehen, einmal gesprochen, und ich liebe sie. Unsere Bahnen gehen weit auseinander, ich bin ihr fern,

4*

ihrem Herzen ein Fremder, und ich liebe sie dennoch! Ich habe sie lieb mit tausend Schmerzen, viel, viel mehr als mein Leben, viel mehr als meine Gedanken, als all mein Dichten und Sinnen — was wäre Freundschaft, was Vaterhaus gegen ihre Liebe? Ich ließe um sie von Gott und Mutter und liebte sie nur mehr! Ja, Bent, das ist meine Liebe, das ist die sturmgeborene Menschenliebe, die echte Liebe — und gerade weil sie so jäh kam, weil sie so tief, so urgewaltig ist, wird sie unglücklich enden."

„Es kann nicht sein!" rief Bent leidenschaftlich. „Du selber glaubst, daß das Leben nach der Vollendung rollt, daß Liebe sein höchstes Moment sei. Sollte das Höchste, was uns gegeben ward, Verderben in sich tragen? Mir würden die Sinne schwinden, wenn ich es glaubte, es wäre entsetzlich!"

„Wenn du ängstlich bist," sagte Versen, „will ich dir einen Rat geben. Liebe niemals, ohne zuvor Eltern und Tanten um Erlaubnis gefragt zu haben. Liebe hausbacken, wenn du den Grad von Glück erreichen willst, der uns vorgeschrieben ist — auch bei der Liebe gilt freilich das Sprichwort: ‚So wie ihr säet, werdet ihr ernten'."

Es lag tiefer Hohn in seiner Stimme. Bent sah ihn groß an, eine qualvolle Frage rang sich in ihm empor.

„Spotte nicht, George", sprach er tonlos. „Kämpft eine erste Liebe nicht alles Erdenweh nieder? Ist eine große Liebe durch den Segen, der in ihr wohnt, nicht rettend für ihre Träger? Vermag sie nicht, hier und im Himmel selig zu machen? Oder lähmt ein Fluch auch sie? Du bist erfahrener als ich, George; antworte mir — ich bitte dich darum bei deiner eigenen Liebe."

Versens Gesicht war finster geworden wie die Märznacht.

„Es ist ein Naturgesetz," sprach er langsam, „daß wir am Übergewöhnlichen, an unseren heftigsten, heißesten Herzensregungen zugrunde gehen müssen."

Unter ihnen lag die Stadt am breiten Strome, die Stadt mit Brücken und Türmen in Nacht begraben, die stillen, verschneiten Dächermassen schimmerten matt herauf. Zuweilen schlug leise eine Turmuhr an, die laublosen Bäume auf der Esplanade schauerten im Tauwind.

„Sieh," sagte Versen, „da unten ist's Winter und alles liegt begraben in letztem Schnee. Sie sollen schlafen. Da plötzlich kommt ein Frühlingsahnen, ein warmer Hauch, ein Märzklang — es brechen die Knospen, welche am sehnsüchtigsten harrten, ihr dunkles Gefängnis. Sie liebten ihn zu sehr, den heiligen Sonnenkuß, sie haben zu jäh, zu früh geblüht. Wohl war das Grün, was sie gebracht, das edelste und schönste vor allem — aber sie haben gefehlt gegen das Gesetz der mählichen Entwicklung, sie müssen sterben in den Tauwassern. So ist es auch mit den Menschen. Der große Haufe blüht, reift, stirbt nach allgemeinen Regeln. Sie lähmt ein mäßiger Frost, ein mäßiger Sonnenblick schafft ihnen Leben — im ganzen haben sie nur Segen davon. Wenn aber ein Herz von sehnsüchtigerem, höherem Schlage zu früh aufgeküßt wird von der urewigen Sonne, wenn es zu jäh erfaßt wird vom Sturm des Schönen, so stürzen bald die Wasser darüber, unwendbar, rächend, gesetzerfüllend. Darum geht ein dunkler Zug durch jedes große Menschenlieben, der Zug des Scheidens, der Zug des Todes. Und nicht wir allein müssen untergehen — auch jene Frau, die wir so sehr geliebt, streift ein dunkler Schatten. Er trifft auch ihre Stirn, sei sie noch so rein, sei sie noch so stolz. Sie wird nie wieder ganz glücklich werden. Vielleicht wird sie hingehen im Glanz des Lebens, jahrelang — einmal wird sie erkennen, daß sie längst gestorben ist, gestorben, ehe sie's selbst gewußt... was ist dir, Bent, deine Hand ist eiskalt?"

„Wenn du beten kannst, George," stöhnte Bent rauh, „so bete für mich."

Er wandte sich kurz und schritt in die Nacht hinaus.

* * *

Als George andern Tages den Freund besuchen wollte, wurde er nicht vorgelassen. Die Wirtin erzählte, daß Bent an nervösem Kopfschmerz litte, sich jedoch geweigert habe, einen Arzt holen zu lassen. „Ich will niemand sehen," hatte er erklärt, als Frau Bitterlich mit einer großen Kanne Fliedertee in sein Zimmer gedrungen, „ich will allein sein, Madame, hören Sie?" Dabei habe er ganz eigentümlich ausgesehen und sogar mit dem Fuße gestampft. Die gute Frau benützte dieses Ereignis, um in eine solche Flut von Klagen über das veränderte Benehmen ihres Mieters auszubrechen, daß George eiligst seinen Rückzug antrat. Als er am andern Tage wiederkam, standen die Sachen noch schlimmer:

Frau Bitterlich erklärte, daß Bent sein Essen kaum berührt und des Nachts ein paarmal ganz entsetzlich gestöhnt habe, jetzt läge er auf dem Sofa und schliefe, der gnädige Herr möge nur selbst durch das Schlüsselloch sehen. Übrigens habe er ihr nicht einmal heute morgen die Tür öffnen wollen, sondern ihr zugerufen, daß es ihm besser ginge, er aber immer noch ungestört bleiben wolle.

George stieg etwas mißgestimmt die Treppe hinab.

Wenn ich ihn unabsichtlich verletzt habe, dachte er bei sich, so ist es nicht hübsch, derart anhaltend zu grollen. Er hat doch eine herbe, fast feindselige Natur, und es ist vielleicht nicht gut, ihm Teilnahme aufzudrängen, so herzlich sie immer sein mag.

Bent lag indessen allerdings auf dem Sofa, den Kopf nach der Wand gedreht, schlief aber nicht. Als die Schritte Georgs verklungen waren, stand er auf, ordnete seinen Anzug und schritt mit höflichem Gruß an der Wirtin vorüber, welche in der Küche mit Tellerwaschen beschäftigt war. Frau Bitterlich hätte vor Erstaunen beinahe die große Suppenschüssel, die sie gerade bearbeitete, fallen lassen, gewann aber doch noch Zeit genug, um ein bitterböses Gesicht aufzusetzen. Als sie jedoch hörte, daß Bent die Treppe hinunterstieg, gewann ihre Fürsorglichkeit die Oberhand. Sie beugte sich über den Pfosten und rief ihm voller Besorgnis nach: er möge wenigstens seinen Schirm mitnehmen, es regne ja draußen ganz furchtbar.

Bent war schon aus dem Bereich ihrer Stimme, er

stand in der Haustür und atmete die kühle Regenluft ein. Die Straße war glänzend schwarz; wo man hinsah, tropfte und plätscherte es von Wasser. Dicht an dem Hause nur war ein schmaler, geschützter Streifen. Bent drückte sich an die nasse Mauer und erreichte vorsichtig die Nebentür, über ihm spien die Dachrinnen Wasserfluten herunter. Die Treppen waren schmutzig, Kistendeckel und lose Bretter standen im Hausflur, zertretene Strohhalme lagen umhergestreut, in den Räumen des ersten Stockwerkes wurde gehämmert, offenbar bereitete man den Einzug neuer Mieter vor. Bent sah im Vorübergehen einen gut erhaltenen ältlichen Herrn im Gespräch mit der Portiersfrau, deren Gesicht vor widerlicher Höflichkeit auseinanderlief; sie neigte den Kopf demütig auf die Seite, plapperte dabei aber so unaufhaltsam, daß es aussah, als ob ihre Lippen sich gar nicht bewegten. Der alte Herr schien Verlangen zu tragen, von ihr fort zu kommen, auf seinem Gesichte lag ein Gemisch von Ungeduld und Höflichkeit, welches hochgestellten Personen eigentümlich zu sein pflegt, und Bent hörte ihn mit nicht lauter, verbindlicher Stimme sagen: „Gut, gut, liebe Frau, machen Sie das alles, wie Sie es haben wollen ... nur recht schön wohnlich, hören Sie, recht wohnlich ..."

„Das Fräulein ist nicht zu Hause," sagte die Magd, indem sie die Tür öffnete, „die Madame ist aber da. Das Fräulein wird gleich aus dem ‚Konversatorium' kommen, soll ich Sie unterdessen melden?"

Bent wollte sich zurückziehen und in Ermangelung

einer Visitenkarte etwas wie ganz ergebene Empfehlungen hinterlassen, allein während er damit beschäftigt war, öffnete sich die Tür und das Haupt von Signora Galieri, mit einer Art von Turban umwunden, erschien in der Öffnung.

„Entra, entra pure," rief sie lebhaft, indem sie ganz hervortrat, „Giacinta wird gleich kommen."

Bent mußte ihr folgen. Sie ging ihm voran in das große Zimmer und ließ sich ächzend in ihre Hängematte nieder, laut klagend, daß dieses verwünschte Wetter ihr Husten, Schnupfen und viel mal di testa zugezogen habe. Es war dunkler im Zimmer wie je, dennoch trug sie zum Schutze der Augen eine große Brille, um sie lag ein Dunstkreis aller möglicher Essenzen und Parfüms, unter welchen Hoffmannstropfen und Patschuli um den Vorrang stritten.

Bent mußte Platz nehmen und ihr klagen helfen. Sie klagte über alles, hauptsächlich aber über sich selbst sowie über den unverzeihlichen Einfall, mit dem Kinde in dieses Land gekommen zu sein, in dieses verwünschte Land, wo die Menschen so plump und alle Dinge ebenso schlecht als teuer wären ... nun habe seit gestern das unglückselige Kind, die Giacinta, den Einfall bekommen, ein Engagement annehmen zu wollen, singen zu wollen um jeden Preis! Sie sei persönlich selbst beim Intendanten des Hoftheaters gewesen — na, der wird sich freilich so etwas nicht zweimal sagen lassen. Hier — ein Engagement! die Silberstimme hin für nichts und wieder nichts ... sie wisse gar nicht, was dem Kinde in den Kopf gefahren sei — gestern habe sie erklärt, daß sie ihr, der Zia, nicht länger zur Last fallen wolle, daß sie frei sein müsse, um ihr, der Zia — ah l'ingrata! zurückzugeben, was sie ihr schuldig — als ob das überhaupt möglich wäre! Und nun bräche das alles über ihr armes, krankes Haupt herein, und dazu in einem Lande, wo alles so teuer (der ganze Klagestrom ergoß sich von neuem), und wo, was ja das allerschlimmste wäre, man keinen Menschen hätte, dem man vertrauen könne, keine Seele, keinen Freund.

Ihre Stimme brach in einer Art von tragischem Achzen, welches man nur auf der Bühne erlernt und welches alten Komödiantinnen leicht zu Gebote steht. Auf Bent verfehlte es jedoch nicht einen tiefen Eindruck hervorzubringen; er stammelte etwas von aufrichtiger Teilnahme und schloß mit der Versicherung, daß unter allen Umständen ein Freund bleiben würde, auf den man sich verlassen könne, und der wäre nämlich er selber.

Signora Galieri fuhr hastig auf.

„O che bravo giovinotto, che nobil' cuore! Aber nein, lieber Freund, tausendmal nein, Sie können uns nicht helfen. Sehen Sie, Sie wissen nichts von all den Dingen, die zu einem ersten Auftreten notwendig sind: die Toilette, die Blumen, die Nebenausgaben — und nein, nein, das wäre ja eine Geldfrage, und die Freundschaft will nichts von Geldfragen wissen ... und doch — hier in dem weiten fremden Lande ist alles so teuer, ach so teuer, und das arme Kind weiß gar nichts davon, daß uns nur so wenig übriggeblieben ist ...“

Sie hatte sich tiefer in die Ecke geworfen und fixierte durch ihre Gläser Bent mit vor Bosheit glitzernden Augen. Wie sie so dalag, glich sie ganz genau einer großen, zusammengeknäuelten Brillenschlange.

„Ich bin arm," sagte Bent rasch, „es kommt lediglich auf die Summe an ... bitte, nennen Sie mir ihren Betrag", fügte er, den Atem anhaltend dringend hinzu.

Sie nahm ein großes, gelbseidenes Tuch, brachte es vors Gesicht und umschlang es dann mit den Händen, als ob sie es ausringen wolle.

„Die Summe," sagte sie endlich so düster, als würde ihr ein furchtbares Geständnis abgepreßt, „die Summe... nun ja, wenn es denn sein muß," sie überflog Bents Persönlichkeit noch einmal mit einem raschen schätzenden Blicke, „nun, hundert Taler müssen es zum mindesten sein, zum allermindesten."

Sie hatte die Worte langsam fallen lassen, damit jedem einzelnen Zeit bliebe, sich in ihrem Munde gehörig mit Gift zu tränken. Wenn sie jedoch gehofft hatte, Bent erbleichen zu sehen, so ward ihr dieser Spaß verdorben. Er rührte sich nicht, nur seine Unterlippe zuckte leise. Wenn sie tausend Taler gefordert hätte, er wäre ebenso ruhig geblieben; war es doch für Giacinta, für Giacinta! Er hob entschlossen das Haupt.

„Ich will die Summe herbeischaffen," sagte er mit fester Stimme, „unter der Bedingung, daß Fräulein Giacinta nie eine Silbe davon erfährt. Es würde ..."

Die Italienerin richtete sich mit einem so hastigen Ruck auf, daß die Stange mit dem Papagei beinahe umgefallen wäre.

„Darüber dürfen Sie ganz ohne Sorge sein," sprudelte sie wütend, „wirklich ganz ohne Sorge, Herr ... Sie caro amico."

Die Tür wurde aufgerissen, das Dienstmädchen stürzte atemlos ins Zimmer und meldete:

„Der Herr Hofrat."

Signora Galieri richtete sich hastig auf, riß den Turban von ihrem Kopfe, wickelte die Brille hinein und warf das Paket in eine Ecke.

„Es kommt Besuch", sagte sie mit einer höchst unzweideutigen Bewegung zu Bent, der ebenfalls aufgestanden war.

In diesem Augenblicke trat der Hofrat ein und die Signora machte tiefe Verbeugungen. Bent wollte hinter dem Besucher die Tür gewinnen, dieser aber maß ihn mit raschem, etwas erstauntem Blicke, streckte den Arm aus und sagte verbindlich:

„Ich hoffe nicht, daß ich gestört habe?"

Bent erkannte den Herrn, den er eine Viertelstunde vorher im Gespräch mit der Portiersfrau gesehen hatte. Er grüßte ehrerbietig und entgegnete, daß der Herr Hofrat keine Störung verursacht habe und daß sein Besuch zu Ende gewesen.

Die Augen des Hofrats streiften die Signora, welche mit allen Merkmalen der Ungeduld auf einen Sessel deutete.

„Sie kennen mich also," wandte er sich wieder zu Bent, „um so weniger könnte ich es verantworten, wenn meine Gegenwart, die nur wenige Minuten dauern wird, Sie vertrieben haben sollte. Darf ich Sie nicht lieber bitten, Madame Galieri, mich mit dem Herrn bekanntzumachen?"

Die Signora lächelte süßsauer. Sie tat zuerst, als ob sie sich durchaus nicht auf Bents Namen besinnen könne, dann brachte sie heraus:

„Herr Sor ... Herr Sor ... Herr Sorenso, Student — wir kennen den Herrn erst seit wenigen Tagen."

„Ich freue mich sehr, Ihre Bekanntschaft zu machen," sagte der Hofrat; „Sie besuchen die Universität schon seit längerer Zeit?"

Man hatte inzwischen Platz genommen; Bent beantwortete die ihm vorgelegten Fragen kurz und bescheiden. Die Signora barst vor Wut, sie behandelte ihren neuen Freund immer ungebundener, wenn nicht zu sagen unhöflicher, indessen der Hofrat mit feinem Takt das Gleichgewicht immer neu herzustellen wußte. Bent bemerkte das alles wohl, hatte aber in seinem Herzen tausend Entschuldigungen für die Signora. Sie lebte ja mit Giacinta so zurückgezogen, es mußte ihr unangenehm sein, daß er mit dem Hofrate zusammengetroffen war ... und dann bewunderte er wieder, wie gut sie ihrem Gaste das heftige Unwohlsein und ihren Kummer zu verbergen wußte, wie sie unaufhörlich scherzen und plaudern konnte. Ja, der Hofrat mit dem gutmütigen feinen Lächeln mußte ein hochgestellter, vornehmer Mann sein — Giacinta selbst hatte es gesagt.

Und plötzlich trat Giacinta ins Zimmer. Sie trug den Mantel überm Arm, in ihrem Haar blitzten Regentropfen; sie grüßte leicht und wechselte mit dem Hofrat einige höfliche Worte. Dann wies sie mit halbem Lächeln auf ihr feuchtes Kleid und wollte das Zimmer verlassen. Aber vergebens. Die Zia hatte sie bereits mit zärtlicher Gewalt an sich gezogen und trocknete ihr unter einem Schwall bedauernder Ausrufe die halb gelösten Flechten. Das junge Mädchen litt es geduldig, aber mit einer Art unheimlicher Gelassenheit; es kam Bent vor, als seien ihre Augen während des ganzen Verfahrens völlig regungslos geblieben.

Der Hofrat scherzte über die zärtliche Sorgfalt der Zia. „Warum in aller Welt haben Sie sich so kühn dem Regen ausgesetzt, Fräulein Giacinta? Am Konservatorium stehen ja Wagen genug! Oder studieren Sie die ‚Undine' jetzt so ernstlich, daß Sie sich praktisch mit Kühleborns Element bekannt zu machen suchen?"

Das junge Mädchen entwand sich langsam den Armen der Signora.

„Ich war nicht im Konservatorium," sagte sie ruhig, „ich komme aus dem Opernhause, wo ich mit dem Intendanten bezüglich meines Engagements zu reden hatte."

„Dio mio!" schrie die Zia tödlich erschrocken; Bent begriff nicht, warum sie erschrak, sie wußte es ja schon lange — der Hofrat ließ betrübt den Kopf hängen und murmelte:

„Also doch."

Giacinta hatte sich aufgerichtet, ihre biegsame Gestalt sah aus, als sei sie aus Stahl geformt.

„Meine Prüfung wird in einigen Tagen stattfinden.

Ich singe zum Klavier eine Arie von Scarlatti und das ‚assis' al piè d'un salice', dann bei vollem Orchester einiges aus ‚Undine'. Mein Engagement hängt von dem Erfolge ab. Und nun bitte ich, mich zu entschuldigen; ich bedarf für die nächsten Tage der vollkommensten Ruhe."

Sie verneigte sich und schritt der Türe zu. Als sie den Vorhang zur Seite schob, wandte sie sich noch einmal um, ihre Augen lagen fest und voll auf Bent.

Es entstand eine kurze, peinliche Pause. Die Signora vermied es, den Blicken des Hofrats zu begegnen, und zerrte in der fassungslosesten Verwirrung an einer Sofaquaste, bis diese abriß. Bent machte Miene, sich zu erheben, der Hofrat unterstützte dieses Vorhaben sofort, indem er aufstand und sich empfahl. Bent wurde gar nicht beachtet, zum Hofrat sagte aber Madame Galieri mit merkwürdiger Betonung:

„Auf Wiedersehen ..."

Dieser reichte ihr etwas zurückhaltend die Hand, welche die Signora mit noch immer niedergeschlagenen Augen hinnahm, dann fiel die Türe zu. Auf dem Vorplatz der ersten Etage stand die Portiersfrau auf der Lauer.

„Herr Hofrat, ich wollte mir gehorsamst die Frage erlauben, ob die roten Gardinen nicht ..."

„Aber, liebe Frau, ich bitte dringend, mich jetzt ungestört zu lassen."

Sie waren auf die Straße getreten, der Hofrat sah prüfend zum Himmel empor, welcher sich wider Erwarten etwas aufgeklärt hatte.

„Ich glaube, wir können zu Fuß nach Hause gehen,

Herr ... Herr Sörensen? Ach ja, entschuldigen Sie; es war wirklich nicht möglich, aus der konfusen Aussprache der Madame Galieri klug zu werden. Haben Sie Zeit und Lust, mich ein Stück Weges zu begleiten? Natürlich, wenn Sie nichts anderes vorhaben."

Bent beeilte sich, der Aufforderung zu folgen, und trat aus angeborener Höflichkeit auf die linke Seite herüber. So gingen sie eine Zeitlang schweigend durch die Straßen, die meisten Menschen, welche ihnen entgegenkamen, grüßten ehrerbietig. Auf dem großen Theaterplatze mäßigte der Hofrat auffallend seinen Schritt und blieb endlich ganz stehen.

„Gestatten Sie mir ein paar Fragen, Herr Sörensen", sagte er mit plötzlichem Entschlusse. „Kennen Sie Frau Galieri und ihre Nichte schon seit längerer Zeit?"

„Nur seit wenigen Tagen," erwiderte Bent, „die Signora hat dieses Umstandes bei meiner Vorstellung erwähnt."

„Hm," meinte der Hofrat, „gerade deswegen wollte ich Sie selbst noch einmal darum fragen. Ich glaube bestimmt, daß Sie viel zu richtiges Gefühl und viel zu gute Erziehung besitzen, um einem ältern Manne, der Sie um eine Aufklärung ersucht, die Unwahrheit zu sagen. Ich danke Ihnen für den Bescheid. Glauben Sie übrigens nicht, daß mich unberufene Neugier leitet — ich will offen bekennen, daß ich für die Damen ein großes und gerechtfertigtes Interesse hege. Signora Galieri war eine berühmte Sängerin, ihre Nichte stammt aus tadelloser, leider sehr armer Familie, beide sind durch ihre

Empfehlungsbriefe an mich gewiesen. Ich darf wohl sagen, daß ich nach Möglichkeit tätig gewesen bin, um ihre Pfade zu ebnen. Ich erwirkte der jungen Dame den Eintritt ins Konservatorium, was wahrhaftig nicht leicht war, indem dort, wie überall in unserem guten Vaterlande, ein feindseliger Zug gegen alles Fremde herrscht. Die junge Dame sollte daselbst noch mindestens ein Jahr lang unter der Aufsicht der Tante ihren Studien obliegen — es war alles so richtig, so natürlich eingeleitet — nun mit einem Male erklärt sie, sie wolle fort von der Tante, sie müsse selbständig werden, selbständig um jeden Preis! Kein vernünftiges Zureden, kein Bitten hilft — als sie der Vorstellungen überdrüssig ist, begeht sie eine Eigenmächtigkeit, läuft zum Intendanten und will durchaus ein Engagement. Es muß etwas in ihr Leben gekommen sein, das sie beeinflußt, das diesen ganzen rätselhaften Umschwung in ihr hervorgebracht hat. Was konnte es aber sein? Sie lebt ja so zurückgezogen! Wenn es ihr jemals gelänge, ein Engagement zu erhalten, so wäre das ein Unglück, ein unausdenkliches Unglück."

Er hatte Bent an einem Rockknopfe gefaßt und sah ihm starr ins Gesicht.

Jener wußte nicht recht, was er erwidern sollte.

„Ich meine," sagte er endlich, „daß sich der plötzliche Entschluß Fräulein Giacintas erklären läßt. Es ist vielleicht in ihr das Bewußtsein eigener Kraft erwacht, sie fühlt sich Künstlerin genug, um ihren eigenen Weg gehen zu können, und wenn es ihr gelingt, was ich fest glaube, so sehe ich nur Schönes und Großes darin, nicht aber etwas Unglückliches."

Der Hofrat stampfte mit seinem Regenschirm so heftig in eine Wasserlache, daß die Tropfen weit umherspritzten.

„Wenn es ihr gelingt, wenn es ihr gelingt," rief er unwillig, „es wird ihr aber nicht gelingen, so glauben Sie mir doch! Ich kenne die Bühne besser wie Sie, und weiß, mit was für Schwierigkeiten eine junge Anfängerin zu kämpfen hat. Sie muß ein Herz von Stahl haben und blind sein gegen alles, was sie umgibt, wenn sie durchdringen will! Viele wenden sich ab vor Gram und Ekel und geben die Sache ganz auf; es sind nicht wenig junge Talente, die der Kunst so entzogen werden. Und dann, haben Sie einen Begriff von den Kabalen, welche einem Debüt vorangehen, gerade diesem Debüt ganz besonders vorangehen werden? Denken Sie doch, eine Fremde, eine Schülerin des Konservatoriums, die mitten aus einem unvollendeten Kursus auf die Bühne eines Hoftheaters springt — das muß ja Aufsehen, Neid, Mißgunst, Tumult aller Art erregen. Ich mag gar nicht weiter daran denken! Natürlich ausverkauftes Haus, bezahlte Opposition, bezahlte Claque, Geschrei und Pfeifen, wütender Applaus ... und in all dem Lärm das arme Kind, ganz allein, ohne eine Idee von Bühnenkenntnis ... es ist wirklich schrecklich, dabei so gar nichts tun zu können, so ganz ohnmächtig sein zu müssen. Können Sie das gar nicht begreifen, Herr Sörensen? Sehen Sie die Sache immer noch in einem so rosigen Lichte?"

Er riß mit nervöser Hast seinen Überzieher auf, auch Bent war sehr erregt.

„Ich kann mir nicht denken,“ murmelte er, „daß ein paar hundert Menschen so feig sein sollten, ein alleinstehendes junges Mädchen zu beleidigen. Und dann bin ich überzeugt, daß Fräulein Galieris Erscheinung ihren Eindruck selbst auf den Rohesten ...“

„Sie täuschen sich gänzlich, junger Mann, Sie täuschen sich gänzlich. Das vielköpfige Ungeheuer Publikum nimmt keine Rücksicht und kennt kein Erbarmen. Es leidet nur das, was nach seinem Geschmacke ist, es will sich für sein Geld amüsieren. Wenn es nicht satt wird, so brüllt es eben. Und was Fräulein Galieris Stimme anbetrifft: wie können Sie nach den wenigen Tagen ihrer Bekanntschaft so genau darüber urteilen?“

„Sie war so gütig, etwas zu singen, als ich der Signora meinen Antrittsbesuch machte“, entgegnete Bent. „Es war ein Frühlingslied, ganz kurz nur, aber so wunderbar süß, daß ich es nie vergessen werde. Sie muß mit dieser Stimme Triumphe erringen, und dann ist sie ja selbst“ — er fügte es aufwallend hinzu — „so stolz wie keine andere, und so bezwingend schön.“

Über das Gesicht des Hofrats lief eine unmerkliche Blässe.

„Ich hatte nie das Glück, etwas anderes von ihr zu hören, als höchst langweilige Etüden,“ sagte er trocken, „aber das genügte mir, um mir ein Urteil zu bilden, welches von dem Ihrigen wesentlich abweicht. Die Stimme ist freilich schön, die Schule tadellos, zuweilen sogar überraschend, aber über dem Ganzen liegt ein böser Schatten, der mich das Äußerste befürchten läßt. Fräulein Galieri hat viel zu früh gesungen. Die Stimme in dieser jungen, kaum achtzehnjährigen Brust ist dem Tode geweiht, nie und nimmer wird sie den Anstrengungen, die ein dauerndes Engagement bedingt, gewachsen sein. Ich fürchte sogar, daß sie nicht einmal die erste Vorstellung durchhalten wird. Die Partie ist gar nicht leicht zu singen, das Haus ist groß, das Orchester stark, endlich muß die Tonbildung des ungewohnten deutschen Textes notwendigerweise erschwerend wirken. Ich für meine Person mache mir über den Ausfall des Debüts nicht die geringste Illusion; es wird ein Unglück geben, lieber Herr Sörensen, was Sie auch sagen mögen. Doch nun habe ich Sie richtig bis zu meiner Haustür mitgeschleppt — entschuldigen Sie, daß ich Sie so lange in Anspruch genommen habe ... das Schicksal der armen Damen geht mir aber wirklich zu nahe."

Ein Türsteher in großem Mantel und dreieckigem Hute hatte das Tor bereits aufgerissen und stand unbeweglich auf dem Hausflur. Der Hofrat wartete, ob Bent noch etwas sagen würde; da dies aber nicht der Fall war, trat er rasch noch einmal auf die Straße und ergriff ihn bei der Hand.

„Lieber Herr Sörensen," sagte er, indem sein Gesicht einen fast kläglichen Ausdruck annahm, „wenn Sie irgend den geringsten Einfluß bei Fräulein Galieri besitzen, so wenden Sie ihn dazu an, sie von ihrem schrecklichen Gedanken abzubringen. Wenn ich Ihnen übrigens von heute ab in irgend einer Weise nützlich oder gefällig sein kann, so verfügen Sie, bitte, über mich in jeder Beziehung. Vorläufig aber will ich mich zurückziehen, ich fühle mich wahrhaft angegriffen."

Er gab Bents Hand frei, trotzdem blieb er unter der Haustür stehen und sah dem rasch Davonschreitenden nach. Als Bent um die Ecke bog, stand der alte Herr noch immer, als ob er etwas vergessen habe, den Hut im Nacken, die Hände tief im modernen Überzieher vergraben, einen hilflosen Zug auf dem wohlwollenden, glatten Gesicht. —

Bent lief nach Hause und schrieb um Geld; es war das erste Mal, daß er's tat. Vor einigen Tagen noch hätte er den Gedanken, seine Eltern um eine Unterstützung anzugehen, als unfaßbar verworfen, jetzt ging ihm der Brief ganz leicht von der Hand. Als er ihn zusiegelte, wußte er sogar kaum, was er eigentlich geschrieben; ihm fiel nur ein, daß es die höchste Zeit sei, denselben abzusenden. Der Zug nach Norden ging um acht Uhr, es fehlten kaum zwanzig Minuten daran. Er lief nach dem Bahnhofe und suchte den Postwagen; als er die Klappe des Briefschalters hob, tönte eben das dritte Signal. Das mahnte ihn an den Tag, wo er an derselben Stelle von seinem Vater Abschied genommen, als der ihn zur Universität gebracht; er sah noch deutlich den strengen Kopf mit den Büscheln früh gebleichten Haares, er hörte auf einmal genau die harte Stimme, welche damals zitterte, als sie sagte: „Gott wird dich segnen, denn du bist ja unsere einzige Stütze" ... er zögerte einen Moment — da, ein greller Pfiff, ein Stöhnen der Maschine — der Brief flog in den Kasten. Dahin polterte der Zug, an Signallichtern vorbei, über Drehscheiben und dröhnende Brücken in die Nacht hinaus. Bent preßte die Lippen fest aufeinander.

„Ich habe euch Kummer bereitet," dachte er, „doch kann ich vielleicht später einmal alles wieder gutmachen."

Er ging langsam zur Stadt zurück. Nun, da das wichtigste Geschäft, der Brief, erledigt war, kam ihm aufs neue die Unterredung in den Sinn, die er so unverhofft mit dem Hofrate gehabt. Er fand die Teilnahme des einflußreichen Mannes für zwei Damen, die ihm empfohlen waren, sehr edel, dessen Besorgnisse in betreff Giacintas Debüt aber viel zu groß. Niemals würden Neid und kleinliche Mißgunst es wagen, die finsteren Arme nach jenem süßen, reinen Geschöpf zu erheben, und wäre es dennoch, so müßten vor ihren sonnigen Augen alle Schatten zu nichts zerfließen; nichts Schlechtes und Gemeines würde davor bestehen können. Und ihre Stimme — wie konnte der Hofrat nur sagen, daß sie gefährdet sei? Würde sie selbst, Giacinta, es nicht am besten wissen? Würde sie, wenn dem so wäre, so gerne singen, so lang und so laut und mit so blühenden Lippen? O, Versen hatte recht — die heilige Lohe brannte auch in ihr, bereit, zum Himmel zu schlagen, um zu leuchten, der ganzen Welt zu leuchten! Sie würde singen, eine Herrscherin sein durch ihre Kunst, eine Königin über alle, und alle würden ihr zujubeln, ihr huldigen, sie anbeten.

Er hielt plötzlich inne, ein trauriges Wort, das einst Giacinta geredet, kam ihm in den Sinn: „Mich hat noch niemand liebgehabt.“ Er sah lange starr vor sich nieder.

„Anbeten ... anbeten ...,“ sprach er leise, „ich glaube, ich hätte etwas Besseres für dich, Giacinta. Ob du auf der Höhe gingest, im sonnigsten Glanze des Glücks, oder ob du arm wärest und verlassen von allen — ich würde bei dir sein und nicht von dir lassen, würde dich im Herzen halten und es keinem sagen, würde mit dir weinen, mit dir lächeln, für dich kämpfen, um dich beten, und fände nie genug daran.“

Er stand am Hause, in dem sie wohnte, es war ganz dunkel. Vom Dache herab tropfte und plätscherte es, zusammen Schnee und Regen, der Märzwind wuchtete an den schwarzen Giebeln.

Er breitete die Arme aus, ein unbeschreibliches Lächeln kam auf seine Lippen.

„Schlaf wohl,“ sprach er leise, „du böses, nie geliebtes Kind, gut' Nacht!“

* * *

Schon am andern Tage lief Bent dreimal auf die Post, um zu fragen, ob kein beschwerter Brief für ihn angekommen wäre. Er wurde ebensooft abgewiesen, endlich gaben ihm die Beamten, da seine Zudringlichkeit ihnen lästig zu werden begann, den Rat, ruhig nach Hause zu gehen und der Geduld zu pflegen, die Briefe würden gleich nach Eintreffen ausgetragen. Er mußte sich fügen, die Zeit jedoch, welche er, von Ungeduld und

Erwartung gequält, auf seinem Zimmer zubrachte, wurde ihm endlos lang. Er versuchte eine Arbeit zu beendigen, die ihm der Maschinenbauer zu schleunigster Erledigung übergeben hatte; beim geringsten Geräusch stürzte er jedoch auf den Vorplatz, kehrte dann enttäuscht zurück und warf die Bogen durcheinander, ohne nur einen Strich getan zu haben. Wenn es dunkelte, stahl er sich auf die Gasse und umkreiste das Haus, welches für ihn verschlossen war, denn ohne Geld hätte er es nie gewagt, vor die Signora zu treten. Bei Tage saß er oft unbeweglich und sah zu, wie die Sonnenstäubchen auf der Diele spielten: er war krank vor Erwartung, seine Nerven waren so überreizt, daß er im Halbschlummer saß und nichts von sich wußte. Aus solch einem Zustande wurde er durch den Postboten erweckt, der vor ihm stand und um Quittung bat. Bent nahm den Zettel, ließ ihn jedoch sogleich wieder fallen und griff nach dem Briefe mit den fünf ungeheuren braunen Siegeln. Erst auf das wiederholte Bitten des Beamten kritzelte er mühsam seinen Namen über den Schein; dann riß er das Kuvert auf und überflog oberflächlich die Zeilen.

„Lieber Sohn!

Du hast uns durch Dein unerwartetes Verlangen viel Sorge bereitet ... ich habe die Ersparnisse Deiner kleinen Schwestern angreifen müssen und doch nicht das Ganze zusammengebracht ...“

Der Brief flatterte auf die Erde, Bent las nicht weiter. Mit bebender Hand wühlte er in den Banknoten; während er sie zählte, setzte sich sein Fuß schwer auf die klaren, etwas zitternden Schriftzüge des Vaters. Er zählte das Paket immer wieder von neuem, er schüttelte mit steigender Aufregung jeden einzelnen Kassenschein — umsonst. Es waren und blieben nur einige achtzig Taler. Was nun anfangen, woher in aller Welt die fehlende Summe nehmen?

Er blieb unbeweglich sitzen. Auf seine Stirn kam ein Zug, der ihm eigentümlich war, wenn er sich über eine unlösbare Formel beugte; sein mageres Gesicht wurde dann immer finsterer und älter, seine Finger flogen einen eigenartig nervösen Tanz. Endlich erhob er sich, trat an das Büchergestell und nahm drei oder vier Folianten herunter, welche er mit einer Art von Ehrfurcht auf den Tisch bettete. Sorgsam reinigte er die schweinsledernen Decken von Staub, dann schlug er zögernd den ersten Band auf. Es war ein berühmtes und selten gewordenes Werk, welches Pastor Sörensen in seinen Studentenjahren erhalten hatte, wegen „tugend- und lobesamen Lebenswandels, nebst fleißiger Inklination zu den Wissenschaften", wie die Hand eines toten Dekans auf das Titelblatt geschrieben. In der obersten Ecke unter den bunten und goldgepreßten Vignetten stand mit kräftigen Zügen: Axel Sörensen, stud. theol., daneben eine halb verwischte Jahreszahl. Dieses Buch war Bents größter Schatz. Es erinnerte ihn an eine der wenigen glücklichen Stunden seiner Jugend, an den Tag seiner Konfirmation, wo ihn der Vater, nachdem er ihm mit eigener Hand das Abendmahl gereicht, in sein Arbeitszimmer gerufen und ihm nach einer kurzen

Ansprache das oft bewunderte Prachtwerk geschenkt hatte. Die Mutter weinte damals vor Rührung, die kleinen Geschwister in ihren Feiertagskleidern starrten den großen Bruder verwundert an, unten wurde das Festmahl gerüstet, und vor dem Pastorate wiegte der dünne Roggen seine grünen Halme im Sonnenschein ...

Bent strich leise mit der Hand über den alten Folianten, dann nahm er eine Schere und schnitt fest und sicher das Titelblatt heraus.

„Du wenigstens", sagte er, „sollst nicht zu fremden Leuten kommen." Dann setzte er seinen Hut auf, schlug mit der Hand darauf, daß er festsaß, und nahm mit einem Ruck die schweren Bücher auf den Arm. „Ihr müßt fort zum Juden," rief er rauh, „es ist nun einmal nicht anders."

Er stürmte zur Tür hinaus. Auf dem Vorplatze saß Frau Bitterlich und schälte Kartoffeln; als sie Bent mit seinen Büchern sah, nickte sie befriedigt.

„Es ist schön," sagte sie, „daß Sie endlich einmal wieder ins Kolleg wollen. Bei dem ewigen Müßiggehen kommt nichts heraus."

Bent war längst die Treppe hinunter. Er ging erhobenen Hauptes durch die Straßen, die Vorübergehenden, die er sonst nie beachtete, sah er fast feindselig an, zuweilen warf er die Bücher herausfordernd von einem Arm in den andern. An der Ecke begegnete ihm Herr von Zierow, ein kleines, sehr geckenhaftes Männchen, welches stets helle Glacéhandschuhe und einen Stock mit ungeheurem elfenbeinernen Knopf trug. Es hüpfte über die Straße, indem es die Lackstiefelchen geschickt auf die trockensten Stellen des Pflasters setzte, und begrüßte Bent mit weicher krähender Stimme.

„Ist's erlaubt, mit Ihnen zu wandeln? Wo gehen Sie hin, teurer Kommilitone?"

„Zum Juden!" rief Bent so laut er konnte, indem er in sehr bezeichnender Weise auf die Bücher schlug.

Von Zierow sah sich entsetzt um.

„Pst, pst, mein Bester", sagte er, indem er sehr gezwungen lächelte. „Also ein wenig in der Klemme und auf einem kleinen Schleichwege, he? Hm, begreife das ungefähr, obschon nie selbst in ähnlicher Lage gewesen, dieu merci. Meine Frau Mutter — und so etwas prägt sich dann fürs Leben ein — pflegte zu sagen: ‚Noblesse oblige, Hippolyt von Zierow! Denk stets daran! Noblesse oblige war seit Jahrhunderten der erhabene Wahlspruch deiner Väter' ... Aber was haben Sie denn, Herr Sörensen, ich wüßte nicht, daß hierbei etwas zum Lachen wäre?"

Bent lachte allerdings, denn sogar ihm, dem Einsiedler, war ganz bekannt, daß die stolze Edeldame, die Stammherrin derer von Zierow, eigentlich eine Buchhalterstochter war, welche einen wohlhabenden Mehlhändler geheiratet. Dieser hatte in den letzten Kriegen durch Lieferungen ein bedeutendes Vermögen und demgemäß bald den Adel erworben; um seinen Hals schlotterte sogar ein großes Verdienstkreuz, welches diejenigen Menschen, die die Ehre genossen, mit Herrn von Zierow näher bekannt zu sein, häufig zu der Bemerkung veranlaßte, daß ein hänfener Strick für den ehemaligen Lieferanten eigentlich ein viel passenderer Halsschmuck gewesen wäre. Deswegen lachte Bent dem kleinen Manne so herzlich ins Gesicht; als dieser aber sich empört zum Gehen wandte, hielt er ihn gemessen zurück.

„Herr von Zierow," sagte er mit sehr ernstem Gesicht, „Sie sind nun Meister einer höchst interessanten Neuigkeit. Wenn Sie erzählten, daß Sie Bent Sörensen, den Tugendspiegel, auf dem Wege zum Leihhause ertappten, und dabei noch ein klein wenig durchschimmern ließen, daß besagter Bent Sörensen schon seit geraumer Zeit einen katilinarischen Lebenswandel führe, so würden Sie mit den Samenkörnern Ihrer Erzählung auf sehr fruchtbaren Boden geraten und auf einige Zeit — wie immer, wollte ich sagen — der Held des Tages sein. Da mir aber nichts daran liegt, daß in drei Tagen die ganze Stadt um meine Verhältnisse weiß, so stelle ich mich unter den Schutz Ihres Zartgefühls, welches bei einem von Zierow ja notwendigerweise feiner ausgebildet sein muß, als bei einem andern, gewöhnlichen Menschen. Ich bin überzeugt, daß mein Geheimnis unter solch einem Schutze gut aufgehoben sein wird, und danke Ihnen schon im voraus für Ihre Verschwiegenheit."

Herr von Zierow tanzte gerade auf zwei trockenen Steinen inmitten der Straße, sein Gesicht trug den behaglich-dummen Ausdruck befriedigter Eitelkeit, obschon sich seine Mundwinkel bei der Zumutung des Verschweigens einer Klatscherei trübselig herabsenkten.

„Seien Sie unbesorgt, cher ami,“ lispelte er, „meine Frau Mutter pflegte zu sagen ...“

„Noblesse oblige“, lachte Bent im Fortgehen, er lachte es laut und höhnisch, weil er wußte, daß Zierow, ein menschgewordenes Tageblatt, lieber gestorben wäre, ehe er eine pikante Neuigkeit verschwiegen hätte. Was liegt daran, dachte er in seiner urwüchsigen, unreifen Selbstironie, die Leute mögen es gerne wissen, ich will mich nicht besser machen, als ich bin.

Bent gefiel sich in dem Gedanken. Als er durch einige Straßen gegangen und seines Weges nicht mehr sicher war, ersah er sich unter den Vorübergehenden einen besonders weltzufrieden aussehenden Bürgersmann, der den Ausdruck behäbigen Philistertums wie eine Legitimationskarte auf der Stirne trug, und fragte ihn, wo das Leihhaus läge. Der Angeredete musterte ihn mit mißtrauischem Blicke, gab wegwerfend Bescheid und entfernte sich überhastig. Bent folgte schweigend der erhaltenen Weisung, ging eine Strecke weiter und bog dann in eine schmale Gasse ein, deren baufällige Häuser den Schmutz förmlich auszuschwitzen schienen. Aus den Fenstern, welche häufig mit Papier verklebt waren, hing gewöhnlich an einem Stocke irgend ein defektes Bekleidungsstück; vor den schmalen schwarzen Löchern, welche die Stelle von Türen vertraten, wälzten und balgten sich notdürftig bekleidete Kinder, deren Köpfe meist einen Überfluß an struppigen schwarzen Haaren zur Schau trugen. Am Ende dieser Häuserreihe lag ein finsteres Gebäude, das wie ein alter Waren=

speicher aussah und ein Schild trug, darauf der Name „Leihhaus", dicht darunter das nichtswürdige Wort: „Mont de piété" zu lesen war. Durch das früh hereinbrechende Dunkel, den Schmutz, die Nässe, durch die vielen schlotternden Gestalten, von denen einige scheu herangeschlichen kamen, andere dagegen so gelassen auf den Eingang zusteuerten, daß man ihnen das gewohnheitsmäßige Betreten dieses Weges ansah, erhielt das Ganze einen abstoßenden Anstrich. Zuweilen kam aus der Tür ein Greis, welcher in Lumpen gehüllt war, und den man seinem schlendernden Gange, seinen halblauten Selbstgesprächen nach als unverbesserlichen Trunkenbold erkennen konnte, dann wieder ein blasses abgehärmtes Weib mit einem Kinde im Arm. Auf diese wartete dann gewöhnlich in irgend einer dunklen Ecke ein Kerl, um ihr das erlöste Geld sofort abzunehmen; man konnte dann noch lange sein rohes Fluchen hören und das leise Weinen der Frau. Bent mußte allen Mut zusammenfassen, um die ausgetretenen steinernen Stufen emporzusteigen. Drinnen war eine große, dämmerige Halle; vor zwei Schiebefenstern, die von einer Öllampe spärlich erhellt waren, drängte sich die Menge. An den Wänden standen und kauerten die seltsamsten Gestalten, Bündel mit Betten und Kleidungsstücken im Arm; durch sie hindurch schritt, in seinen Regenrock gehüllt und sich anscheinend sehr teilnahmlos umsehend, ein Schutzmann. Die Unterhaltung wurde meist im Flüsterton geführt, in einer Ecke nur hatten einige abschreckend aussehende Weiber ein Stück Leinenzeug ausgebreitet und keiften darum;

manchmal auch wurde das allgemeine Summen durch das laute Schluchzen einer Unglücklichen unterbrochen, welche mit ihrem kleinen, wertlosen Paket gänzlich abgewiesen worden war; über dem Ganzen lag ein unbeschreiblich widerlicher Geruch von Laster und Armut.

Bent blieb mit den Büchern im Arm fassungslos an einem Pfeiler stehen. Wie um Gottes willen sollte er den Schwarm, welcher die Schiebefenster belagerte, durchdringen können? Und es wurde schon Abend — heute, da er die Mittel dazu besaß, mußte er Giacinta sehen, er mußte es, denn er fühlte, daß sonst die künstliche Anspannung, welche ihn in den letzten Tagen aufrechterhalten, zu Ende gehen würde. Er preßte sein Taschentuch vor den Mund und versuchte, sich von der Menge an das Gitter hinanschieben zu lassen, doch war es umsonst. Stets wurde er, in solchem Unternehmen ungeübt, nach der Wand zurückgeworfen. Zum Äußersten entschlossen, begann er Gewalt zu brauchen; das einzige, was er erreichte, war, daß man ihm einige gemeine Schimpfworte zurief. Verzweifelnd wollte er umkehren und versuchen, an einem andern Punkte durchzukommen, als er sich plötzlich am Ärmel gezupft fühlte und niederblickend einen kleinen, fettigen Juden vor sich sah, der ihm mit blöden, zwinkernden Augen zuwinkte, in eine Ecke zu kommen. Er ließ sich nicht abweisen, sondern zwinkerte und lispelte fortwährend:

„Lassen Sie uns reden, lassen Sie uns reden ... hab' ich doch gleich gesehen, daß Sie sind ganz was Apartes, weil Sie haben einen Widerwillen gegen die armen Lait, und gesehen hab' ich auch, daß Sie nicht werden durchkommen vor Abend und vielleicht Geld haben müssen und 's nicht kriegen werden, so wahr ich heiß Veit Itzig und ein ehrlicher Mann bin. Und da hab' ich mir gesagt: Veit Itzig, obschon du sonst nicht machst leicht ein Geschäftchen, so willst du doch tun ein'n Gefallen dem jungen Mann und ihn fragen ..."

In Bents Augen kam ein Strahl von Hoffnung.

„Sie könnten mir allerdings einen großen Gefallen tun," sagte er hastig, „ich muß heute abend fünfzehn Taler haben, und wenn Sie diese Bücher dafür nehmen wollten ..."

Er konnte nicht ausreden. Kaum hatte der Jude das Wort „Bücher" vernommen, als er zurückprallte und mit dem Ausdruck der größten Enttäuschung die Hände erhob.

„Bücher," wehklagte er, „Bücher haben Sie gesagt? Waih, wie bin ich doch gekommen mit meinem Vertrauen an den unrichtigen Mann! Wo wollen Sie hin mit die Bücher, wenn Sie nicht gehen zum reichen Reb Chaim Samuel, der da ist ein mächtiger Sammler und wohnt Sternstraße siebenzehn, drei Treppen hoch? Waih mir, daß ich verloren hab' mein' kostbar' Zeit mit so viel Geschmuse, wobei nicht 'rauskommt der kleinste Profit."

Des Juden Antlitz belebte sich plötzlich. Seine Augen waren an Bent hinuntergeglitten und an der Uhrkette hängen geblieben, welche unter dessen Rock hervorsah.

„Gott der Gerechte," sagte er mit gänzlich veränderter Stimme, „hab' ich doch gleich gewußt, daß der Herr will haben zum besten den armen Veit Itzig! Wie kann man doch wollen treiben Handel mit Büchern, was ist meschugge Ware, wenn man hat im Sack eine Uhr, was ist reelles Metall. Hab' ich's doch gleich gedacht, der Herr wird dir geben was zu verdienen, weil du gehabt hast das gute Herz und hast ihn gerissen 'raus aus die arme Lait, wohin nicht passen tut ein feiner Herr und ein nobler Herr; weil du ihn hast gerissen 'raus, nicht um zu machen mit ihm ein Geschäftche, sondern nur um ihn zu erretten aus seiner großen Verlegenheit."

Bent hatte gar nicht an die Uhr gedacht; es war ein wahrer Glücksfall für ihn. Mit rascher Handbewegung riß er sie samt der Kette aus der Tasche und brachte so den Redeschwall des Juden zum Verstummen. Dieser machte sofort mit seinen dürren Fingern das Gehäuse auf, rieb an der Kette und hielt sie ans Licht, während sein Gesicht einen immer mißbilligenderen Ausdruck annahm.

„Ist eine alte Uhr, eine schlechte Uhr," brachte er endlich hervor, „ist abgegriffen das Silber und ramponiert die Kett'. Ist ein schlechtes Stück Arbeit und gereicht nicht zur Ehre solch einem feinen Herrn. Aber gleichviel, hat doch der alte Veit Itzig ein gutes Herz, und weil er will retten den Herrn aus der großen Verlegenheit, will er ihm geben vier Talerch bar, ob er auch sein wird ein geschlagner Mann und es heißen wird: der Veit Itzig ist gewesen wie immer das Opfer von seinem guten Herz und wird ewig bleiben ein armer Schacherjüd. Nehmen Sie hin die vier Talerch," fuhr er heftiger fort, als er sah, daß Bent etwas entgegnen wollte,

„nehmen Sie sie hin oder es gereut mich weiß Gott und ich kann nicht nehmen mehr die Uhr und der Herr wird müssen warten und wird kriegen kein Geld mehr heut' abend, zu kommen heraus aus seiner großen Verlegenheit."

Das Gebot war ein unverschämtes. Die alte Uhr, durch drei Predigergenerationen vom Vater auf den Sohn gegangen, besaß allerdings keinen großen Wert, dennoch mußte der würdige Itzig trotz seiner Beteuerungen mindestens das Doppelte daran verdienen. Bent fühlte das auch, da er jetzt aber fürchtete, für seine Bücher nicht so viel erhalten zu können, als er gehofft, ließ er mit schwerem Herzen die Kette fahren, worauf sie sowohl als die Uhr in eine der weiten Taschen des Juden verschwanden. Dieser zog sodann einen Lederbeutel hervor und begann ein Päckchen unglaublich schmutziger Kassenscheine aufzuwickeln, von denen er unter vielem Seufzen Bent vier der zerrissensten überreichte, jedem einzelnen Klagen über das schlechte Geschäft, welches er gemacht, und über seine grenzenlose Gutmütigkeit, die ihn dazu verleitet, nachsendend.

Das Gesicht des menschenfreundlichen, biedern Veit Itzig bekam plötzlich einen merkwürdig blöden Ausdruck, während er seinen Kragen einzog und den Kopf instinktmäßig zwischen den Schultern verbarg. Diese Erscheinung fand ihre alsbaldige Erklärung darin, daß der Schutzmann, welcher schon einigemal scharf herübergeblickt hatte, jetzt gemütlich auf ihn zukam und ihn mit kurzem Kopfnicken anredete.

„Guten Abend, Moses," sagte er mit der freundlichsten Stimme von der Welt, „es freut mich, daß ich dich schon wieder einmal abgefaßt habe. Du wirst es hoffentlich noch einmal weit bringen, Moses."

Dem Juden war offenbar höchst unbehaglich zumute. Er verbeugte sich demütig vor dem Schutzmann, sprach einiges von „großmächtigem Herrn Polizeirat" und begann dann von seinem Edelmute zu reden, der ihn dazu getrieben, einem jungen, höchst bedürftigen Manne einen Dienst zu erweisen. Dabei schlug er unaufhörlich die Augen zum Himmel und machte ein so unschuldiges Gesicht, daß man hätte schwören mögen, Herr Veit Itzig, von zuverlässigerer Seite jedoch Moses benannt, sei der uneigennützigste Mensch unter der Sonne und schlechterdings unfähig, sich auf Kosten seiner Nebenmenschen um nur eines Hellers Wert zu bereichern.

„Schon gut, edler, verkannter Moses," unterbrach ihn der Schutzmann, „du wirst aber ebenso genau wissen wie ich, daß es dir verboten ist, deine sauberen Geschäfte hier zu treiben, solange du unter Polizeiaufsicht stehst. Ich habe dich heute zum zweitenmal ertappt — erwische ich dich zum drittenmal auf faulem Pferde, so ist es fürs erste aus mit dir. Und nun, lieber Moses, tu mir den Gefallen und schere dich fort, wenn du nicht willst, daß ich dir Beine mache."

Moses ließ sich das nicht zweimal sagen, er tauchte förmlich unter in der Menge. Der Schutzmann sah ihm einen Augenblick nach und sagte dann finster zu Bent:

„Wird Sie gut betrogen haben, der alte Gauner. Hat schon mindestens zehn Jahre wegen Hehlerei und Wechselfälschung gesessen. Hätten sich auch an einen Bessern wenden können.“

Bent war wie betäubt. Die Hitze, der im Saale brütende Dunst nebst dem Anblick von so viel Schmutz und Elend raubten ihm fast den Atem. Er stürzte hinaus und rannte in eine belebtere Straße, nur um in eine andere Umgebung zu kommen. Die Bücher hingen schwer in seinem Arme und schnitten ihm ins Fleisch, sie mahnten ihn zunächst daran, daß er sie ja los werden müsse, daß er noch nicht Geld genug habe. Er blieb einen Augenblick stehen und besann sich. Der Jude hatte ihm die Adresse eines Antiquars genannt — er hatte sich einen Augenblick daran festgeklammert als letzte Hoffnung — dann war aber der andere Handel dazwischen gekommen. Er sann eine Minute bang nach ... als Mathematiker fiel ihm zunächst die Hausnummer ein, siebenzehn ... Gott sei Dank, er hatte es: Reb Chaim Samuel, Sternstraße siebenzehn.

Reb Chaim Samuel verschob den Schirm seiner Lampe, so daß ihr Licht voll auf Bent fiel. Reb Chaim hatte einen Ahasverkopf mit silberweißem Haar, er trug ein Käppchen von Samt, seine hohe, gebeugte Gestalt sah in dem faltigen Hauskleide ehrwürdig aus. Das Gemach war sehr dunkel, nur den schweren eichenen Tisch umgab Lichtflut, auf ihm stand ein seltsam geformtes Trinkgefäß voll rotem Wein. Daneben lagen Bücher und eine Handvoll antiker goldener Spangen.

Diese raffte der Jude mechanisch zusammen, das Klirren des Goldes in seiner zitternden Hand begleitete die dringenden, bewegten Worte, mit denen Bent sein Anliegen vorbrachte.

„Lassen Sie sehen", sagte Reb Chaim mit tiefer Stimme. „So", er schob die Spangen achtlos beiseite, schlug den ersten der schweren Bände auf und vertiefte sich in die Vorrede. Nach einiger Zeit stand er auf, nahm von einem Nebentische ein Heft und begann langsam darin zu blättern. „Ich kann Ihre Bücher nicht brauchen," sagte er endlich, „wie ich eben sehe, besitze ich bereits eine ältere Ausgabe des Werkes."

Es war Bent, als ob ihm die Kehle zugeschnürt würde. Er trat einen Schritt vor und breitete die Bücher nebeneinander aus, er schlug sie auf und klappte sie wieder zu, seine Hände zitterten dabei.

„Ich beschwöre Sie, Herr Samuel," sagte er, „nehmen Sie die Bücher dennoch, ich trenne mich selbst unendlich schwer von ihnen. Ich verlange ja nur elf Taler dafür und sie sind gewiß mehr wert. Wenn Sie sie nicht kaufen wollen, so leihen Sie mir das Geld darauf, ich bin an Arbeit gewöhnt und werde nicht ruhen, bis ich Ihnen alles abbezahlt habe. Das Opfer ist Ihrerseits so klein, und Sie könnten mit so wenigem einen Menschen glücklich machen."

„Ich bin kein Pfandverleiher," sagte der Jude rauh, „wenn ich etwas kaufe, so behalte ich's auch. Und was das Glücklichmachen anbetrifft, so ist das Gefasel für Narren und Kinder. Sie kennen mich schlecht, daß Sie gerade vor mir dieses Wort ausgesprochen haben. Reb Chaim Samuel reicht nur Steine, er reicht kein Brot mehr. Doch nun genug, Herr, sparen Sie sich das Weitere, ich mag Ihre Bücher nicht kaufen."

Bent stand einen Augenblick wie vernichtet, dann überkam ihn eine unsägliche Bitterkeit.

„Mein Gott," sagte er dumpf, „das ist also die Nächstenliebe und das sind deine Menschen!"

Aus Samuels Augen schoß ein Blitz, seine Gestalt reckte sich zu ihrer vollen Höhe.

„Menschen!" schrie er wild, „Menschen? Ich bin kein Mensch, ich bin nur ein Jude! Sie gilt nicht für mich, eure Nächstenliebe! Euch sollte ich lieben, euch, die ihr verfolgt habt unseren Stamm rastlos durch die Jahrtausende, die ihr ihn verfolgt noch immer, nicht offen, denn ihr beugt euch unserem Golde, aber heimlich, mit allen Waffen des Hasses und der Verachtung? Euch sollte ich lieben, die ihr gezwungen habt unser Volk zur Entartung, daß es verdirbt in seinen Palästen und daß es umkommt in seinen Hütten vor Schmutz und Elend, wie ein unreines Tier? Euch sollten wir Gutes tun, die ihr gemacht habt aus unserem großen Volk ein verlorenes Volk? Ich kenne keine Nächstenliebe, ich kenne nur den Haß! Und das schwöre ich beim Gott meiner Väter, der ein großer Gott ist und ein gewaltiger Gott: ich hasse euch alle tief und bitter, ich hasse euch mit dem letzten Atemzuge, der meinen morschen Körper durchzittert! Von meiner Tür will ich euch weisen im Leben und euch verfluchen in meiner Todesstunde, so wahr mein

Gott ein Gott der Rache ist und so wahr ich selbst ein Jude bin. Von meiner Schwelle, Christ! Ich hasse alle die Deinen."

Reb Chaim hatte den Arm erhoben und seine Augen flammten; er sah schön aus in seiner Begeisterung.

Bent gewann bei diesem plötzlichen Ausbruch einer großen Leidenschaft seine volle Ruhe wieder, er trat kurz an den Tisch und nahm seine Bücher.

„Entschuldigen Sie mein Drängen," sagte er, „ich sehe nun, daß ich Ihnen nicht länger beschwerlich fallen darf. Mein Kommen entschuldigt sich von selbst, denn es brachte Ihnen Gelegenheit zu einer guten Tat. Eine solche hat nichts mit Glaubensverschiedenheit zu schaffen, sie adelt alle Konfessionen und bringt immer Segen. Leben Sie wohl."

Er grüßte höflich und wandte sich zum Gehen, der Jude stand noch immer unbeweglich und starrte in das Leere.

„Er hat recht, Vater, erfülle seinen Wunsch", sagte plötzlich eine weiche, unendlich müde Stimme.

Reb Chaim fuhr zusammen, als habe ihn eine Kugel getroffen, auch Bent wandte sich um. Er sah eine seltsame Erscheinung. Die Tür eines Nebenzimmers, zu dem einige Stufen führten, war leise aufgegangen, silberne dreiarmige Leuchter warfen einen breiten Lichtstreifen ins Gemach. Mitten in dieser Helle stand ein junges Mädchen, gelblichblaß, mit großen, sonderbar blickenden Augen. Sie trug ein buntschillerndes Seidenkleid, um den Kopf eine Art von Turban, unter diesem quollen einige Strähnen wundervollen blauschwarzen Haares hervor und fielen auf den ganz entblößten Hals nieder. Mit ihrem linken, durchsichtig magern Arm hielt sie sich am dunklen Türvorhang fest, mit dem rechten drückte sie eine vor Liebkosungen halbtote Taube an ihre Brust, ihr brennend roter Mund war halb trotzig, halb weinerlich gespannt.

Des Juden hohe Gestalt war bei diesem Anblick gänzlich zusammengebrochen, mit ausgestreckten Händen wankte er auf das junge Mädchen zu.

„Miriam, mein Kind", flehte er angstvoll. „Habe ich dich im Schlaf gestört? Hat dich meine Heftigkeit erschreckt? Fühlst du dich kränker wie sonst? Sprich doch, Kind, du marterst mich, wenn du nicht sprichst."

„Ich habe gar nicht geschlafen, Vater", sagte das Mädchen mit derselben müden, schleppenden Stimme. „Das Kind", sie deutete auf die Taube, „war so unruhig und wollte umhergetragen sein. Dann habe ich dich reden hören, o, du warst böse ... und dann hat der junge Mensch etwas gesagt, das war ganz recht und sehr schön ... was war es doch? Ach ja: eine gute Tat bringt immer Segen ... und da wollte ich dich bitten, lieber Vater, seinen Wunsch zu erfüllen, wir brauchen ja den Segen so sehr, schon um des Kindes willen."

Aus den Augen des alten Mannes rollten ein paar große Tränen, die er umsonst zu verbergen suchte.

„Gewiß, Miriam, meine einzige Miriam," sagte er mit erstickter Stimme, „ich tue alles, was du willst, und das" — er wandte sich zu Bent — „tue ich besonders gern. Ich bitte Sie," flüsterte er in flehendem Tone, als er sah, daß Bent abwehren wollte, „lassen Sie mir die Bücher, mein Kind würde sich sonst ängstigen und aufregen. Verzeihen Sie, was ich über Ihre Glaubensgenossen gesagt habe, und tragen Sie mir es nicht nach — sehen Sie," fügte er ganz leise hinzu, „es war ja auch ein Christ, der mir mein Kind getötet hat."

Bent war tief erschüttert, er nickte nur leicht und ließ die Bücher auf den Tisch gleiten, dabei sendete er verstohlene Blicke nach dem Judenmädchen hinüber. Das stand noch immer regungslos an der Tür und wartete auf den Ausgang des Handels.

„Diese Bücher, mein Herr," nahm jetzt Samuel lauter das Wort, „sind mehr wert als elf Taler, ich bin in der Lage, Ihnen das Doppelte bieten zu können." Dabei nahm er aus einem Fache des Tisches eine Handvoll Silbergeld. „Nehmen Sie nur," sagte er wehmütig lächelnd, als Bent sich weigerte, „nehmen Sie getrost: so viel gibt Ihnen ganz gewiß jeder Jude."

Bent zählte elf Taler ab und schob den Rest mit einer Handbewegung, die keinen Widerspruch duldete, zur Seite.

„Nehmen Sie heißen Dank," sprach er tiefbewegt, „und möge Sie, mein Fräulein," — dabei trat er einige Schritte auf das Mädchen zu — „der Segen Ihrer guten Tat umschweben; möge er Ihnen ein Glück bringen so rein und schön, wie Sie selbst es sind."

„Du," sagte das Mädchen, „wecke nicht mein Kind. Aber komm her — höre, du hast gewiß eine Braut?

O, dann habe sie sehr lieb und verlasse sie nicht, hörst du, niemals! Ach, das ist gar zu schrecklich ..."

Sie schauderte zusammen und preßte ihre Hand gegen die Stirn. Bent wandte sich zum Gehen; Reb Chaim Samuel saß, den Kopf in die Hände vergraben, sein hagerer Körper bebte vor Schluchzen. Das Mädchen hatte sich auf die Stufen gesetzt, wiegte die Taube in ihrem Arm und summte ein hebräisches Wiegenlied. —

Draußen begann man die Laternen anzuzünden, der Regen hatte aufgehört. Bent eilte seiner Wohnung zu, das Geld hatte er in der Brusttasche geborgen, sein Herz klopfte daran. Was er in den langen Nachmittagsstunden erlebt, lag überwunden im Nebel; der Gedanke, für Giacinta etwas getan zu haben, benahm ihm jedes traurige und peinliche Gefühl, er war einzig vom Glücke des Wiedersehens erfüllt. Sie sitzt jetzt wohl am Klavier, dachte er, und ihre Hand geht leise über die dämmernden Tasten, denn die Zia ist, wie stets, gegen Abend eingenickt. Allmählich werden die Akkorde klarer, und aus dem dunklen Vorspiel löst sich vielleicht jene Weise voll Veilchenduft und Jugendsonnenschein: „O primavera, gioventù di vita ..." und sie hält inne und stützt das Köpfchen in die Hand und flüstert leise: Warum ist er nur so viele, viele Tage nicht gekommen?

Das Blut schoß ihm zu Kopfe, er bemühte sich, noch schneller zu gehen. Er wollte, ehe er Giacintas Wohnung betrat, noch einmal nach Hause, um seine Hand zu waschen, die Moses, der Zuchthäusler, berührt. Er rieb sie heftig und lange, tauchte auch seine Stirn, die ihn schmerzte, in kaltes Wasser; dann atmete er hoch auf und stieg die Treppe zu Madame Galieris Wohnung hinan.

Er war sehr erstaunt, die Entreetür weit offen zu finden, Möbel und Wirtschaftsgeräte waren im Gange höchst unordentlich aufgetürmt, einige Weiber hantierten unter lautem Schwatzen mit Wasser und Scheuerbesen. Als Befehlshaberin dieser Schar erwies sich die Portiersfrau, welche Bent unaufgefordert mitteilte, daß die gnädige Frau schon seit einigen Tagen in der ersten Etage wohne, das Fräulein habe jedoch ihr Zimmer im vierten Stock vorläufig beibehalten.

„Ach ja," schloß sie ihre Rede, „es war auch hier oben für die gnädige Frau nicht vornehm genug. Der Herr Hofrat haben das von jeher gesagt."

Einige der Weiber begannen hierbei verstohlen zu kichern. Bent war dieser plötzliche Wechsel nicht ganz klar, er stieg nachdenklich ins erste Stockwerk hinunter und zog die Klingel. Das Dienstmädchen öffnete ihm, stieß, ohne ein Wort zu sagen, eine Flügeltür auf und rannte in die Küche zurück. Bent blickte mit Erstaunen in einen prächtigen Salon voll seidener Möbel, Topfpflanzen und Statuetten. In dem großen kristallenen Kronleuchter brannten rosige Wachskerzen, durch die schweren Fenstervorhänge fiel das letzte Licht des Tages. An einem Tische, der mit Büchern und Notenheften bedeckt war, saß Giacinta. Als sie den Eintretenden bemerkte, erhob sie sich und streckte ihm langsam den Arm entgegen.

„Bleiben Sie an der Tür," sagte sie mit gänzlich ruhiger, leidenschaftsloser Stimme, „bleiben Sie an der Tür, ich bitte Sie darum. Dieser Ort taugt nicht für einen ehrlichen Mann."

Bent blieb stehen, er hielt seine Augen irr und entsetzt auf sie geheftet.

„Sie verstehen mich nicht?" sprach sie mit zuckenden Lippen. „Ich glaube es wohl. Sehen Sie, alles das" — sie deutete mit einer fieberhaften Bewegung auf die prachtvolle Umgebung — „ist nicht unser. Ein anderer hat es bezahlt. Sein war alles, wovon wir seit Wochen gelebt haben, er hat alles bezahlt, alles. Ich sollte verkauft werden, langsam verkauft, und hab's zu spät gewußt ... ich habe das Aufgeld bekommen, hübsch nach und nach, damit ich's nicht merken sollte. Nun aber bin ich sehend geworden und will es zurückzahlen mit Zins und Zinseszins! Heute entscheidet sich alles ... wie könnt' ich die Schmach sonst fassen und ertragen? In einer Stunde ist meine Prüfung. Mir ist gar nicht bange, nur meine Brust schmerzt mich sehr; ich muß aber singen, heute besser wie je, um jeden Preis! O, Bent," rief sie plötzlich leidenschaftlich aus, „es kann ja vielleicht noch alles gut werden! Nicht wahr, Sie, mein einziger Freund, glauben fest an mich und vergeben mir, was ich getan, vergeben mir, daß ich im Unwissen so schwer gefehlt habe?"

Er hatte bis dahin am Türvorhange gestanden, angeklammert wie ein betrunkener Mann. Jetzt stürzte er auf Giacinta zu und bedeckte ihre Hand mit Küssen.

Diese Hand war glühend, die schmalen Finger zuckten und flogen.

„Gehen Sie," sagte sie mit ihrer süßen, ruhigen Stimme, „ich will Sie an diesem Orte nie wiedersehen. Beten Sie, daß Gott in der nächsten Stunde mit mir sei, sonst —" sie neigte das Haupt und sagte so leise, daß er es nicht verstehen konnte: „werden wir uns niemals wiedersehen."

Sie schritt langsam durch den weiten Saal der Türe zu. Bent stand schwankend da, die Gedanken brausten in seinem Kopfe. Schon mehreremal hatte er in einer Ecke etwas wimmern und verbissen schluchzen hören, jetzt entdeckte er die Signora, welche, einem Klumpen gleich, das Haupt in Decken vergraben, auf einem Sofa lag. Ihm kam unklar und verwischt der Gedanke, daß sein Geld vielleicht eine große, unbestimmte Gefahr abwenden könne. Unter dem Vorwande, sich nach ihrem Befinden erkundigen zu wollen, näherte er sich und schob leise wie ein Dieb seinen Schatz unter die Decke.

Die Signora zuckte auf, ergriff das Päckchen und schleuderte es nach Bents Haupt. Das Papier barst und öffnete sich; die schmutzigen Scheine flatterten weit umher, die Silbermünzen rollten kaum hörbar über den kostbaren Teppich.

Giacinta wandte sich um. Ihr Mund wölbte sich zu einem Zuge unsäglicher Verachtung, dann senkte sie still das Haupt.

„Bent," wiederholte sie, „beten Sie für mich."

Er ging auf sein Zimmer, setzte sich an den Tisch und

vergrub die Stirn in beide Hände. Er wußte nun alles, es war wie ein Blitz, der ihn angerührt, aber der Strahl hatte ihn geblendet, er war keines Gedankens, keines Entschlusses fähig. Sein Kopf war heiß und schwer, es raste darin, ihn überkam eine Art von Bewußtlosigkeit. Im Zimmer war es ganz dunkel, zuweilen glitt ein schwacher, eilender Schimmer über die Wände und das rasche Rollen eines Wagens tönte herauf, dann wurde es wieder still, nur der Märzwind schnob heftig über die Dächer. Bent dachte: „Du willst schlafen, vielleicht verschläfst du Herzeleid und Weh und wachst nie wieder auf." Dann vergingen ihm die Sinne wirklich. In sein Ohr kam ein Brausen wie von stürzendem Wasser, vor seinen Augen braute es wie Nebel — und in dem Nebel ward eine Helle, darin stand ein blasses Mädchen, einen Veilchenkranz im wehenden Haar, die dunklen Augen nach oben gerichtet. Sie sagte einfach und traurig: „Nun bin ich ganz allein." Allein ... es riß ihn jäh empor, daß er aufgerichtet stand und nur den einen Gedanken festhalten konnte: sie hat keinen auf der Welt als dich und sie muß dein werden, dein für ewig, du stürbest denn sonst. Dann war es ihm wieder, als sei Giacinta gestorben, als höre er Glocken, die durcheinander klangen, dazwischen die letzten Worte: Bete für mich. Er raffte sich auf, brach mitten im Zimmer in die Knie und wollte beten. Er konnte es aber nicht, er brachte nichts heraus als: Giacinta ... Gott ... erbarme dich unser — und unablässig gingen die Glocken, darüber hin brausten tausend Stimmen wie ein de profundis...

Er wachte plötzlich ganz auf. Der Wind drückte gegen die Scheiben, vom Johannisturm schlug es elf Uhr, alle Glocken riefen es verworren nach. Eine unsägliche Angst überkam ihn: das Schicksal Giacintas, sein Schicksal, mußte sich ja schon längst entschieden haben. Er öffnete das Fenster und sah in die leere Gasse hinab, dann schloß er es wieder mit fester Hand.

„Es muß ein Ende haben," sagte er, „es ist nun alles gleich."

Aus seinem Schreibtische nahm er den Bodenschlüssel, den er seit seinem letzten Zusammentreffen mit Giacinta nicht mehr aus der Hand gegeben hatte, und schritt die Treppe hinauf.

Oben klapperten die Ziegel, ein blasser Mondstrahl fiel durchs zerklaffte Gebälk, bei dem unsichern Lichte sah er, daß die Dachtür verschlossen war. Er blieb einen Augenblick davor stehen, dann schmetterte er sie mit einem furchtbaren Schlage aus den Angeln, daß sie sich in der Luft drehte und krachend in den Hof niederschlug. Er lachte laut hinter ihr her; Wildgänse, die dicht über den Dächern zogen, hoben sich mit hellem, vielstimmigem Geschrei; unten wurde Licht.

„Die Türe ist heruntergefallen", hörte er sagen, dann ward alles stiller als zuvor, der Wind allein fing sich in der Öffnung und wuchtete an dem ächzenden Dache.

„Frühlingssturm", rief Bent laut, dann sprang er mit einem Satze auf die Terrasse herab. Die Blumen, die Giacinta gepflegt, neigten sich und flogen, die Ranken des Efeus flatterten zerwühlt und gelöst wie schwarzes

Frauenhaar. Sie umrahmten einen niedrigen Eingang, von dem ein paar Stufen herabführten, dann kam eine Biegung des Ganges und eine einzelne Tür ... Bent legte die Hand auf das Schloß und tat einen Schritt vorwärts. Er befand sich in einem großen Zimmer, das sein Licht von einer einzigen Lampe erhielt, welche in rosigem Gehäuse an der Decke hing. In der entferntesten Ecke war eine Wolke von weißem Spitzenstoffe, der das Bett verhüllte, sie war genug auseinandergeschoben, um ein Madonnenbild erkennen zu lassen, hinter welchem Myrtenzweige steckten. Auf dem Tische, unter den weichen Strahlen der Lampe, lagen einige Buketts von Märzveilchen, welche einen frischen, tiefbetäubenden Duft verbreiteten, ein weißer Spitzenschleier war lässig daneben geworfen. Am Fußende des Bettes hing ein Kreuz aus Elfenbein, davor kniete, den Kopf auf beide Arme gelegt, Giacinta.

Sie sah nicht auf bei dem leisen Geräusch der Tür, es war nur, als ob ein leises Zittern ihre Gestalt durchliefe. Bent stand schwer atmend und unbeweglich, die Hand aufs Herz gepreßt.

Endlich erhob sie sich. Sie war noch im Undinengewande, von starrer, mattsilberner Seide umflossen, Wasserrosen im dunklen Haar. Sie hatte viel geweint und in ihren Augen blitzten Tränen, aber da hindurch brach ein Sonnenstrahl von Unschuld und tiefem Glück.

„Wir sind gerettet, Bent", sprach sie mit unbeschreiblich glückseligem Lächeln.

Er tat einen Schritt vorwärts und taumelte zu ihren

Füßen nieder, seine Stirn vergrub sich in ihrem Kleide, seine Brust hob sich vor Schluchzen und Stürmen.

„Giacinta, ich liebe dich", brach es aus seinem Herzen, und es klang wie Frühlingsstimmen und Quellen im März.

Er war erlöst. Ehe sie ihn noch geküßt, fühlte er ihre Tränen auf seiner Stirn. Er sprang auf und umschlang sie fest, dann führte er sie zum Fenster und riß es auf. Der Tauwind brach herein und schlug die warmen Schwingen um die beiden, dann brauste er hin und sang um die Giebel sein Auferstehungslied. Bent hatte ihr lockiges Haupt an seine Brust gedrückt, in den Sturm der Frühlingsnacht hinein rief er ein Gebet aus seines Herzens Tiefe, wilde, kindische, glückselige Worte.

Am Himmel rasten dunkle, zerrissene Wolkenmassen über den Mond, das Wasser tropfte von allen Dächern. Ihre Lippen blühten auf seinem Munde, ihre Blumenaugen leuchteten in die seinen.

Sie löste sich plötzlich aus seinen Armen.

„Was ist dir, Giacinta, mein Glück, meine Seele, mein Weib?"

Sie antwortete nicht, ihre Brust hob sich schweratmend, sie preßte die Hände vor die Augen.

„Bent," sagte sie, „wir sind zu glücklich! Wird uns Gott darum nicht zürnen?"

„Gott?" rief Bent, aufjubelnd. „Gott gab uns unsere Liebe, Gott rettet uns aus der Trübsal, befrage ihn darum ..."

Auf dem Tische lag eine Bibel. Bent schlug seine

zitternde Hand in die Blätter, er tat einen einzigen Griff, dann las er mit bebender, metallischer Stimme:

„Mein Gott, betrübt ist meine Seele, drum denke ich an dich — deine Fluten rauschen daher, daß hier eine Tiefe und da eine Tiefe brausen; all deine Wasserwogen und Wellen gehen über mich ..."

„Gott will uns trösten, Geliebte, will uns erlösen" —

Er ließ das Buch fallen und stürzte auf Giacinta zu, seine Arme umschlangen sie wild. Ihren schmiegsamen Leib durchlief ein Schauer, dann brach sie auf seinem Herzen zusammen.

Über sie hin gingen die Tauwasser.

* *
*

Als Bent am andern Morgen erwachte, war sein Kopf kühl und klar, seine Brust voll berauschender Seligkeit. Die Sonne schien seit lange zum erstenmal, lachend fiel sie in das graue Stübchen, vergoldete die tannenen Regale, malte Lichtringe an die Decke, streifte schräg die Kante eines ehrwürdigen Buches, füllte das ganze ärmliche Zimmer mit Gold und Licht. Er kleidete sich hastig an und rüstete seine Büchermappe, seine Augen leuchteten, er lächelte zuweilen selig vor sich hin. Draußen war wundervolles Tauwetter, ein Rauschen und Rieseln, Sonnenschein und frischer Wind, der Schnee schmolz von den Dächern, blitzende Tropfen fielen aufs glänzend schwarze Pflaster. Er ging langsam über die Esplanade der Universität zu, ganz wie ein Träumender; die Fülle reizender Bilder, die in ihm aufgegangen war, erschien ihm übermächtig. Es war ja plötzlich so viel Glück gekommen! Was hatte das eine Jahr, welches vor ihm lag, das eine Jahr voll Arbeit und Mühe noch zu bedeuten? Giacinta und er waren beide so jung und liebten sich so sehr, alles Leid, aller Zweifel waren ja zu Ende, sein Leben nun sonnenklar. Das Examen? Pah! Er lachte auf und reckte sich, als gälte es, einen schweren Stein zu heben. Dann dachte er weiter, an das stille Pfarrhaus im Norden, an sein gutes Mütterchen mit dem frühgebleichten Haar, an den ernsten Vater, der aber gewiß lächeln würde, wenn der Sohn mit seiner jungen, hocherrötenden Frau zum erstenmal ins Zimmer träte. Dann wäre ja alles gut. Alle wären versorgt und geborgen. Wie würden die kleinen Geschwister jubeln, was würde das für ein Leben im Pfarrgarten sein! Um die Hecken herum, über Wege und Beete ginge die wilde Jagd, und mitten unter den Kindern würde ein junges Wesen sein, eine zweite Mutter, leuchtenden Auges, lachend vor Lust und Glück ...

Und da war sie wirklich. Aus einem Seitenwege, der die Allee kreuzte, kam sie leichten Schrittes, in einfachem, dunklem Kleide, ankämpfend gegen den Frühlingswind; sie ging gerade auf Bent zu und grüßte ihn mit hellem Lächeln.

„Es freut mich," sagte sie, „daß du so früh ans Werk gehst. Aber komm, du hast noch eine halbe Stunde Zeit und ich möchte dir einiges sagen. Gib mir deinen Arm und höre mich an."

Sie gingen tiefer in eine der Seitenalleen. Die Anlagen waren fast menschenleer, zuweilen nur begegnete ihnen ein Briefträger oder ein paar Bäckerjungen; die wunderten sich wahrscheinlich über den Studenten, der an einem Arme eine so schöne junge Dame führte, während er mit dem andern seine große Büchermappe ängstlich festhielt.

Bent ging schweigend neben Giacinta, er konnte sich an ihr nicht satt sehen. Sie war anders geworden, es lag etwas so allerliebst Sorgliches in ihrem Wesen, in der ganzen Art und Weise, mit der sie ihren Plan für das nächste Jahr entwarf. Sie wollten ihre Verlobung fürs erste geheimhalten, sie würde mit der Familie des Oberregisseurs, der ein sehr braver Mann sei, wohnen, Bent dürfe sie nicht alle Tage sehen — nein, ganz gewiß nicht, „es würde dich von deinen Studien abziehen" — und lernen, immer mehr lernen wolle ja auch sie, geteilte Arbeit sei halbe Arbeit, und es wäre ja eigentlich doch schön, daß sie ihr Glück nicht blind hinnehmen, sondern es erst tüchtig verdienen müßten.

Bent fühlte sich in diesem Augenblicke schon glücklich genug, er hörte kaum, was sie sagte. Eigentlich war es ja auch gar nichts Wichtiges, sie hatte ihm nur mit feinem Takt am Morgen, am frischen, klaren Morgen begegnen wollen.

„Du mußt gehen, Bent," sagte sie plötzlich, indem sie ihren Arm aus dem seinen löste, „es ist hohe Zeit. Nimm auf den Weg, der uns allein zum Ziele führen kann, auf den Weg zur Arbeit den ersten Segenswunsch und den ersten Kuß deiner Frau."

Sie bot ihm frei, ohne zu erröten, die frischen Lippen und ging die Allee hinunter. Bent starrte ihr nach; er glaubte noch immer ihre Stimme im Ohre zu haben, es war aber nur ein Frühlingsvogel, der sich über ihn auf einen Zweig gesetzt hatte und so laut sang, als wolle er sich die kleine Brust sprengen. Etwas weiter davon hatte ihr Kleid den Schnee hinweggestreift, grüne Blätter lugten scheu hervor. Bent wühlte nach und fand zwei winzige, noch fest verschlossene Veilchenknospen; er pflückte sie ab und tat sie in eine Mappe, dann ging er mit langen Schritten der Universität zu. Eine ruhige Sicherheit, eine unwiderstehliche Arbeitskraft waren über ihn gekommen, er sehnte sich nach Hindernissen, nach scharfen Problemen, nach Schwierigkeiten, er fühlte sich siegesgewiß und stark wie ein Gott.

Als er in den Hörsaal trat, hatte der Vortrag soeben begonnen. Nach schüchternem Gruße wollte er seinen alten Platz, dicht unter dem Katheder, einnehmen, fand ihn aber von einem andern besetzt. Zwanzig Köpfe wandten sich nach ihm um; Bent glaubte, in den Gesichtern neben allgemeinem Erstaunen auch Neugier und Schadenfreude zu entdecken; er setzte sich verlegen auf eine der hintersten Bänke und vertiefte sich in den wiederaufgenommenen Vortrag. Was sein Mißbehagen noch vermehrte, war die Wahrnehmung, daß es ihm geradezu schwer wurde, den Deduktionen und Schlüssen des Professors zu folgen, er fand Lücken in seinen Heften und konnte sich kaum zurechtfinden, es kam ihm vor, als seien seine geistigen Fähigkeiten, sein sonst so rasches Auffassungsvermögen eingerostet. Er war froh, als die Stunde zu Ende war. Die Studenten klappten geräuschvoll ihre Hefte zu, der Professor blieb im Hinausgehen an Bents Platze stehen und sagte:

„Ein Wort, Herr Sörensen, wenn ich bitten darf."

Er war ein alter Mann, Bent reichte ihm Hut und Überzieher von der Wand herunter und folgte ihm schweigend durch die langen, weißgetünchten Gänge. In diesen, sowie in den Türen der Hörsäle standen Studenten und plauderten während des akademischen Viertels; Bent sah viele Bekannte darunter und wechselte Grüße mit ihnen, es war ihm aber, als ob auf allen Gesichtern derselbe befremdende Ausdruck läge, als ob hinter ihm ironisches Flüstern und unterdrücktes Gelächter laut würde. Im Konferenzzimmer angelangt, legte der Professor seine Bücher auf den Tisch und wandte sich um. Seine Gebärde war knapp, sein Gesicht streng geworden.

„Vorläufig", begann er, „ist es nichts Offizielles, was ich Ihnen zu sagen habe. Ich spreche überhaupt sehr selten mit jungen Leuten, und nur mit solchen, die sich meines Interesses würdig gemacht haben. Fähigkeit ist Ihnen nicht abzustreiten, dafür können Sie freilich nichts — daß Sie dabei aber fleißig waren und Ihren Eltern eine Stütze zu werden suchten, achte ich. Sie waren bei weitem mein bester Schüler; Ihre geistreichen Kommilitonen nannten Sie deswegen den Tugendspiegel. Das ist immer gefährlich; wer hoch steht, fällt am tiefsten. Sie haben es plötzlich für überflüssig erachtet, das Kolleg zu besuchen; Sie haben, wie Sie sich dessen öffentlich gerühmt, Ihre Habseligkeiten im Leihhause und bei Juden feilgeboten — unnütz zu sagen, daß dieser Umschlag bei Ihnen ganz besonders auffallen mußte. Das waren zwei Punkte. Über den dritten, der natürlich das Motiv Ihrer Ausschreitungen ist, will ich nicht reden, weil ich nichts Bestimmtes weiß. Ihre Kommilitonen werden darüber wahrscheinlich desto unterrichteter sein. Haben Sie die Güte," fuhr er fort, als Bent eine Einwendung wagen wollte, „mich ausreden zu lassen. Mir sind schon so viel junge Leute durch die Finger gegangen, daß ich genau weiß, ob die Worte, welche ich freilich meist nutzlos an sie verschwendet habe, gerechtfertigt sind oder nicht. Die Hauptsache — und das ist der Zweck unserer ersten Unterredung — ist, Ihnen zu raten, energisch umzukehren. Hoffen wir, daß Ihnen der Rückweg gelingen, und daß mich nie der zweifelhaft angenehme Auftrag treffen möge, Ihnen das consilium abeundi mitteilen zu müssen, wozu Sie vorläufig meiner Ansicht nach weit reifer sind, als zum Staatsexamen. Beherzigen Sie meine Mahnung, Sie können gehen."

Er wandte sich ab, Bent rang vergeblich nach Worten, das Gehörte war zu unerwartet, zu plötzlich gekommen.

„Ich danke für Ihre Teilnahme, Herr Professor," sagte er endlich, „auch ich hoffe zum letztenmal der Gegenstand derselben gewesen zu sein."

Dann stand er draußen auf dem kahlen weißen Gange, die Studenten saßen bereits wieder in den Hörsälen. Er war froh, daß er keinem mehr begegnete, ihn überkam ein plötzlicher Widerwille vor jenen jungen Leuten, er fand sie unreif, kindisch und roh dabei. Er fühlte, daß er in wenigen Tagen um Jahre gealtert sei; es wurde ihm klar, daß er nicht mehr in ihre Mitte passe. Es kam die Strafe dafür, daß er eigene Wege gegangen, daß er sich von Lustbarkeiten und Gelagen so philisterhaft ferngehalten hatte. Bent fand beinahe ein Lächeln und faßte den Entschluß, sich in Zukunft noch mehr zurückzuziehen und sich eine Art von Einsamkeit zu schaffen, damit er unbeobachtet und vor Neugier gesichert leben könne. Dann kam ihm ein Gedanke, der ihn stutzig machte. Was hatte der Professor mit dem dritten Punkte, von dem er geredet, bezeichnen wollen?

„Ihre Kommilitonen", so lauteten seine Worte, „werden darüber wahrscheinlich bereits im klaren sein." Seltsam — sollte vielleicht eine neue Klatscherei, etwa gar eine Verleumdung dahinter stecken?

Er fühlte sich nicht mehr fähig, den übrigen Vorträgen beizuwohnen, sondern beschloß, nach Hause zu gehen und dort zu arbeiten. Wie er um die Ecke des Ganges bog, hörte er eine Stimme, die ihm wohlbekannt war, und die ihn bewog, einen Augenblick stehen zu bleiben. An der Tür des Laboratoriums sah er eine Gruppe angehender Mediziner in blauen Kitteln und Leinwandschürzen; in ihrer Mitte stand, geschniegelt wie immer, Herr von Zierow. Er sprach eifrig und die anderen hörten ihm so andächtig zu, daß keiner Bent bemerkte.

„Nun kommt aber noch das beste, meine Herren",

krähte das Männchen. „Wir alle wissen, daß unser teurer Kommilitone, der Ex-Tugendspiegel, durch eine unbekannte Dulzinea vom Wege zur mater alma, den er früher mit Eifer und als leuchtendes Vorbild für uns alle zu wandeln pflegte, auf bedenkliche Weise abgeleitet worden ist. Meinen rastlosen Nachforschungen — denn Sie können mir glauben, meine Herren, daß ich ein ganz besonderes Interesse an den Tugendspiegel wende — ist es nunmehr gelungen, den Schleier zu lüften. Die Glückliche, welcher es gelang, das Kunststück zu vollbringen, ist ..."

Er sah sich triumphierend im Kreise um.

„Nun?" riefen ein halbes Dutzend Stimmen auf einmal.

„Reb Samuels Tochter, der verrückte Judenbalg aus der Sternstraße."

Ein brüllendes Gelächter erhob sich. Der Erfolg war groß, Herr von Zierow wand sich ordentlich vor Seligkeit.

Durch die Lachenden schritt plötzlich Bent. Er grüßte nicht und sah keinen an, nicht einmal Herrn von Zierow, der einen furchtbaren Schreck bekommen hatte. —

Zu Hause angelangt, arbeitete Bent mehrere Stunden; als er fertig war, ging er zu Frau Bitterlich hinüber und bat um etwas zu essen. Die Frau schien aber nicht ihren guten Tag zu haben, denn sie entgegnete, daß sie geglaubt, Herr Sörensen speise seit einiger Zeit auswärts, demzufolge sei bei ihr nichts vorrätig. Bent wartete, bis es dunkel geworden, und ging dann aus;

unten angekommen, blickte er zu Madame Galieris Fenstern empor, konnte aber nicht den kleinsten Lichtschimmer entdecken. Giacinta mußte demnach wohl schon beim Oberregisseur wohnen. Da sind auch wieder Kämpfe und Tränen gewesen, dachte er im Weitergehen — armes Lieb, dir wird der Weg noch schwerer gemacht als mir.

An der Ecke war ein hell erleuchteter Bäckerladen, das weckte seinen Hunger von neuem. Er kaufte ein paar Brötchen und einige Früchte, schlich in eine Seitengasse und aß im Gehen. Die Straße mündete in den Opernplatz, er sah das große Gebäude plötzlich vor sich liegen. Es hob sich massig vom dunklen Hintergrunde ab, über der Freitreppe flackerten schwache Gasflammen ängstlich im Winde, sie warfen Streiflichter auf zwei riesengroße Zettel, welche die morgige Vorstellung ankündigten. Bent trat mit Herzklopfen näher ... da stand es ja wirklich: Undine, romantische Zauberoper in vier Aufzügen, Fouqué, Albert Lortzing ... dann Berthalda, Tochter Herzog Heinrichs, Ritter Hugo von Ringstetten, Kühleborn, ein mächtiger Wasserfürst — Undine — und statt des Namens drei Sterne. Unten kamen die drei Sterne wieder und da stand: „Fräulein Giacinta Galieri als erster theatralischer Versuch." Wie sah das alles so tot und kalt aus, wie waren die drei Sterne so regelmäßig, wie waren die Buchstaben so entsetzlich steif und schwarz! Bent ging traurig weiter, es hatte ihn peinlich berührt, den Namen Giacintas öffentlich gedruckt und allen Blicken preisgegeben zu sehen. Er sagte sich wohl im stillen, daß es ja gar nicht anders sein könne, daß es eine Notwendigkeit sei, er schalt sich hundertmal selbst einen Toren — umsonst, der trübe Eindruck wollte nicht weichen. So kam er an der Hofbuchhandlung vorbei; viele Menschen drängten sich an das Schaufenster. Im Vorbeigehen sandte er mechanisch einen Blick nach den hellen Scheiben und blieb stehen, regungslos, wie zum Tod erschrocken. Drinnen waren Bücher blau und rot, mit fettem Golddrucke ausgestattet, dann Photographien berühmter Männer, der Fürst des Landes, Schopenhauer, Bismarck, unser Fritz, auf Wörth anreitend; im Vordergrunde aber, vom Reflex der Spiegelscheiben überblendet, ein wundervolles Kabinettsbild, versehen mit einer unausstehlich schönen Frakturunterschrift: Giacinta Galieri. Das Bild war sprechend ähnlich, doch lag ein eigentümlich fremdartiger Hauch darüber, es hatte einen Zug, der unerklärlich war und zum Raten aufforderte. Es war ein originelles Zusammentreffen von Trauer, Ergebung und Hohn, es war ein süßes Kindergesicht, dessen Anblick eigentlich weh tat. Bent war mit einem Satz im Laden. Durch den drückenden Papiergeruch schwamm ihm ein elegant gekleideter, süß lächelnder Jüngling entgegen und frug nach dem gefälligen Begehren. Nachdem er dieses vernommen, öffnete er das Schaufenster, hackte mit einer geschäftigen Bewegung das Bild vor den Nasen der Außenstehenden hinweg und begann es in Seidenpapier einzuwickeln.

„Siebzehn und einen halben Groschen, wenn's gefällig ist", lispelte er.

Bent suchte allerhand Münze zusammen und entrichtete den geforderten Betrag, dann ergriff er hastig das Bild und ging zur Tür hinaus. Alle Neugierigen, welche draußen standen, sahen ihm mit unfreundlichen Blicken nach; er achtete nicht darauf, sondern rannte seiner Wohnung zu, er wollte allein sein mit dem Bilde. In seinem Kopfe brauste es. Wie konnte so etwas vorkommen, wie durfte das mit Giacinta geschehen? Wußte sie darum und war es so ihr Wille? Unmöglich. Und vielleicht doch ... es war am Ende so Brauch, es war wohl eine Notwendigkeit, unvermeidlich, aber bitter. Wie gut, daß gerade er noch zurecht gekommen, um der Schaustellung ein Ende zu machen! Wie freute er sich, das Bild in sein armes Stübchen tragen zu dürfen; wie war er glücklich, es nun für immer den Augen der Neugierigen entzogen zu haben!

Der arme Junge! Wäre er fünf Minuten später an demselben Laden vorbeigegangen, so hätte er ein neues Bild von Giacinta auf die Straße lächeln sehen. Wäre er noch ein wenig länger geblieben, so hätte er mit ansehen müssen, wie Herr von Zierow nebst mehreren Genossen ans Schaufenster trat, das Bild für deliziös erklärte, es kaufte und es in die Schublade tat, die er zuweilen nach einem guten Diner seinen Freunden geheimnisvoll zu eröffnen pflegte, und in der die große Zahl seiner auf ähnliche Weise gemachten Eroberungen ruhte.

Am andern Morgen erhielt Bent einen Brief, der folgendermaßen lautete:

„Da ich seit vierzehn Tagen vergeblich auf die Ablieferung der Ihnen anvertrauten Arbeiten gewartet habe, so ersuche ich Sie nunmehr, mir die betreffenden Stücke, ob vollendet oder nicht, umgehends zurückzusenden. Aus allerhand Gründen, deren Erörterung wohl überflüssig sein dürfte, muß ich Sie zugleich bitten, die mit mir geknüpften Verbindungen als gelöst betrachten zu wollen.

Siemers, Maschinenbauer."

Bent war schmerzlich überrascht, er rollte die allerdings unfertigen Berechnungen zusammen und trat den weiten Weg nach der Vorstadt an. Er wollte den Maschinenbauer selbst sprechen und eine bestimmte Erklärung von ihm erbitten. Es mußte irgend ein Mißverständnis vorgefallen sein; auf den zwar eigenen, aber gerechten und wohlwollenden Mann konnten ein paar müßige Klatschereien doch unmöglich großen Einfluß ausgeübt haben. Er hoffte, daß wenige Worte genügen würden, um eine Verständigung herbeizuführen. Zu seinem großen Erstaunen wurde ihm aber gesagt, daß der Maschinenbauer ausgegangen sei und erst in einigen Stunden zurückkommen würde. Nach Ablauf dieser Zeit erhielt er ähnlichen Bescheid und gab nun mit schwerem Herzen seine Papierrolle ab. Als er traurig fortging, glaubte er am Fenster das Gesicht der Frau zu erkennen, welche ihm nachsah, sich aber sofort zurückzog; gleich darauf lief ihm der kleine Sohn des Maschinenbauers, der soeben aus der Schule gekommen war, nach und gab ihm die Hand. Bent strich liebkosend über den hübschen, flachsblonden Scheitel des Knaben.

„Es ist gut, daß ich dich sehe, Paul," sagte er, „ich werde nun wohl lange nicht wiederkommen. Weißt du nicht, warum dein Vater so böse auf mich ist?"

„Nein," antwortete der Knabe, „aber neulich beim Abendessen hat er mit der Mutter über dich gesprochen. ‚An dem Gerede und meinen paar Plänen liegt mir nichts,' meinte er, ‚es steckt aber noch mehr dahinter.' Als die Mutter dich dann verteidigen wollte, hat er mir und der Anna geheißen, spielen zu gehen, und als wir nach einer halben Stunde wiederkamen, saß die Mutter ganz still da, und ich glaube, sie hatte auch geweint."

Bent entließ das Kind und wandte sich zum Gehen. Des Knaben Worte waren ihm unerklärlich und unverständlich geblieben, dennoch fühlte er sich traurig gestimmt. Er machte einen langen Umweg über das Glacis und die Esplanade, wo ihm gestern Giacinta begegnet. Es dunkelte bereits, schmutzigbraune Schneehaufen hoben sich unbestimmt vom durchweichten Boden ab, dann und wann kam eine schwarze Wasserlache; ein starker Wind schüttelte die nackten Bäume in den Anlagen. Er ging weiter auf der anderen Seite des Stromes, bis die einbrechende Nacht ihn zwang, zurückzukehren. In den Vorstädten brannten schon einzelne Lichter, dann kamen die breiteren Straßen, die ganz hell waren. Von der Brücke, welche beide Stadtteile verbindet, warfen helle Gasflammen ihr Licht in den Strom, Bent lehnte sich müde ans Geländer. An ihm vorbei liefen die Leute eiliger als sonst, Wortwechsel und aufgeregte Stimmen wurden laut, Feuerwehrwagen rasselten mit kurz gellendem Glockenschlag übers Pflaster. Gleich darauf kamen ein paar Kompagnien Infanterie, die Offiziere trugen Regenmäntel und hohe Stiefel, die Leute marschierten ohne Tritt und lebhaft plaudernd; anstatt der Gewehre hatten sie Schaufeln und Hacken über der Schulter, eine Schar von Neugierigen lief hinter ihnen her.

„Was ist's, was gibt's?" riefen viele Stimmen.

„Eisgang und Deichbruch", scholl es herüber. „In Annenau hat's die Brücke weggerissen, das Dorf ist in Gefahr, alle Saaten liegen tief unter Schollen und Tauwasser."

Tauwasser! Das Wort schlug Bent mitten ins Herz. Es mahnte ihn an Versens letzte Worte, die er kaum verstanden, und die ihn doch so tief erschüttert hatten. An jenem Abend freilich war seine Seele noch dunkel gewesen, die stürzenden Gewalten in ihr rangen noch nach Entfesselung. Nun war das Eis gebrochen, nun war er gekommen, der heftige frühe Sonnenkuß — und nun brausten auch die Tauwasser einher, eine wilde Sturmflut, alles begrabend, junges Grün, junges Glück, ihn und sie, rächend, vernichtend, gesetzerfüllend ...

Der Wind war stärker geworden, er raste warm und feucht über den Wasserspiegel, er strich wuchtig über die dunklen Dächer der Stadt und drohte die Gasflammen zu löschen, die sich in ihrem Glaskäfig wanden wie verdammte Seelen. Ihre Streiflichter überflogen Bent, der regungslos in der Nacht stand. Sein Haar flog im Winde, er hatte die Augen irr zum Himmel erhoben.

„Wenn wir gefehlt haben," stöhnte er, „so treffe es

mich, mich allein — mit ihr doch, allewiger Gott, habe Erbarmen. Zerschmettere mich, aber habe Erbarmen mit ihr."

Der Himmel war schwarz, kein einziger Stern sah herab. Stromaufwärts zuckten einzelne Lichter, kreuzende Punkte im Nebel; unten war ein Rauschen und Gurgeln, das Wasser schoß unheimlich durch die Brückenbogen, dunkle grünkantige Massen kamen pfeilschnell getrieben, verschoben sich knirschend oder zerbrachen klingend an den Pfeilern.

Drüben im Dunste der Stadt ward eine Helle, die sich mehr und mehr ausbreitete. Sie kam vom Opernhause her, wo man heute abend Lortzings „Undine" gab.

Das Haus war glänzend besetzt. An den Treppen, welche zu den Hoflogen führten, standen Schildwachen, das Gewehr bei Fuß, in den Gängen und Garderoben herrschte reges Treiben. Drinnen war ein Knistern von Seide, ein Aufleuchten von weißen Schultern und funkelnden Steinen, ein warmer Lichtglanz, ein erwartungsvolles Summen; in das Ganze warf zuweilen eine Violine ihre prüfenden, blitzhellen Gammen. Der Abend bot doppeltes Interesse; abgesehen davon, daß „Undine" als Lieblingsoper der Fürstin neu ausgestattet in Szene ging, sollte neben der Debütantin, einer Schülerin des landesherrlichen Konservatoriums, der berühmte Bariton Rossi als einmalige Gastrolle den „Kühleborn" singen.

Auch auf der Bühne herrschte mehr Leben und Aufregung als sonst. Maschinisten und Arbeiter hatten mit dem Stellen der schwierigen Dekorationen vollauf zu tun, hier und da standen Feuerwehrleute in blitzenden Messinghauben, ganz oder erst halb kostümierte Choristen schrien nach Friseur und Theaterschneider, durch das Gewühl schritten einige Bevorzugte, denen das verbotene Paradies der Kulissen zugänglich war. Unter diesen befand sich der Hofrat, welcher sichtlich aufgeregt mit dem Intendanten sprach.

Seitab vom Gedränge, in einer hell erleuchteten ruhigen Ecke, standen die meisten der Mitwirkenden, bereits im Kostüm ihrer Rollen. Auf einem Versatzstücke saß Pater Heilmann in voller Ordenstracht, dies verhinderte jedoch nicht, daß sich eine allerliebste kleine Bäuerin mit blauen Zwickelstrümpfen höchst unbefangen auf seinen Knien wiegte. Vor einem Wandspiegel weilte, in Bewunderung seiner selbst versunken, der lyrische Tenor, ein süßlicher Bursche, der früher Kellner gewesen war. Ein Barett mit riesenhaften Straußfedern zierte sein strohgelbes Haupt, an seine fetten, nach innen gebogenen Beine, die er oft liebevoll betrachtete, schlug ein großes Schwert in roter Samtscheide. Veit, der gemütvolle Schildknappe, stand daneben und fluchte, weil ihn der Bügel seiner Armbrust auf die Nase geschlagen hatte. Herzogin Berthalda, vulgo Frau Lydia Müller, rauschte soeben im grünsamtnen Jagdgewand aus ihrer Garderobe.

Sie war eine schöne, üppige Frau, der das blonde Haar im goldfarbigen Netze nicht übel stand; sie hatte aber kein angenehmes Lachen, und wenn sie lachte wie jetzt, unaufhaltsam, aus voller Kehle, so verlor sie entschieden. Es lag etwas Gewaltsames in ihrer perlenden Lachskala, was weder fröhlich noch gut klang.

„Denken Sie sich, Rossi," sagte sie, indem sie an den übrigen vorbeiging, ohne sie im mindesten zu beachten, „wie ich in die Garderobe der kleinen Galieri komme, um mir ihre Toilette anzusehen, sitzt die neue Diva zwischen ihren Pomadetöpfen und Schminktiegeln, hat ein Kreuzchen, oder einen Fetisch, oder Gott weiß was in den Fingern, starrt ins Leere und gibt kaum Antwort, wenn man sie anredet. Sie sah so einfältig aus, daß ich mich nicht halten konnte und ihr laut ins Gesicht lachte. Ich bin noch ganz echauffiert! Nicht wahr? Fühlen Sie nur einmal."

Der Angeredete war ein schlanker Mann, der, in seinen Mantel gehüllt, schweigend an einem Versatzstück lehnte. Er zuckte mit keiner Muskel, als Frau Lydias weiche Hand seine Wange streifte, er nahm die Zärtlichkeit hin, so wie man die Tabakswolke eines übervertraulichen Nachbars erträgt.

„Wenn Sie Ihre Lustigkeit für sehr begründet halten," erwiderte er in reinem, leicht fremdartigem Deutsch, „so lachen Sie nur nach Herzenslust. Zeit genug haben Sie dazu, Signora. Sie arbeiten" — er betonte das Wort ganz unnachahmlich leicht — „ja erst im zweiten Akte."

Die Sängerin schien über den kühlen Empfang etwas betroffen.

„Ich wäre auch gewiß nicht so früh vor Ihr gestrenges

Antlitz gekommen," entgegnete sie mit einem hübsch studierten Schmollen, „wenn es nicht eben das Debüt wäre, von dem ich um keinen Preis nur so viel" — sie schnippte leicht mit den Fingern — „verlieren möchte. Ich bin wahrhaftig nicht schadenfroh, dennoch gäbe ich etwas darum, wenn die Kleine mit der Engelsmiene und dem dünnen Stimmchen Fiasko machte, schon damit sie sähe, wie weit man mit Hochmut und ein paar Gebeten kommt. Ich kann nun einmal solche Tuerei nicht leiden. Ma foi, da haben wir's doch anders angefangen! Als ich debütierte — ich glaube als Page in Gott weiß was —, hatten wir gerade eine Landpartie gemacht, bei der wir uns köstlich amüsierten. Ich hatte das ganze Theaterelend vergessen; als der Vorhang aufging, wußte ich keinen Takt, kein Wort von meiner Rolle — aber es ging doch famos, die Herren Offiziere applaudierten ganz ungeheuer, und nachher hatten wir irgendwo ein großes Souper, bei dem es so lustig herging, daß ich am andern Tage nicht wußte, wie ich eigentlich nach Hause gekommen war. Jedenfalls habe ich mich zwölf Stunden lang nicht gerührt und bin erst wach geworden, als mir die Mama das Morgenblatt mit einer ganz famosen Kritik ins Bett brachte. Das war ein Debüt, flott und so wie's in der Ordnung ist. Meinen Sie nicht auch, Rossi?"

„Es war wenigstens charakteristisch für Sie, Signora Müller", erwiderte er. „Sie gingen rüstig und ungeniert ans Handwerk ... bravo, dafür sind Sie auch eine ausgezeichnete Sängerin geworden."

Sie sah mit gesenktem Kopf und halb geschlossenen Augen zu ihm empor.

„Sängerin? Nur Sängerin? Das war ein armes Kompliment, Rossi. Ich weiß zwar, daß Ihr Urteil streng ist, dennoch hatte ich gehofft, ein anderes Wort zu hören. In jeder Kritik, die man mir sendet, steht es zehnmal mindestens, aber gerne hätte ich's auch einmal aus Ihrem Munde vernommen. Es könnte mir zwar ganz gleich sein, wie Sie über mich denken, aber", fügte sie kaum hörbar hinzu, „das ist leider nicht der Fall, und Sie wissen gar nicht, Rossi, wie viel ich von Ihnen halte ..."

„Sie dachten hoffentlich nicht, daß ich sagen würde, Sie seien eine Künstlerin geworden, Signora", sagte der Sänger, indem zum erstenmal eine leise Regung in sein Gesicht kam. „In diesem Falle hätten Sie sich geirrt, da ich auf einem veralteten Standpunkt stehe und ganz absonderliche Ansichten hege. Es ist ein eigenes Ding um die Kunst, man zieht sie nicht an wie ein seidenes Kleid, zehn Minuten ehe der Vorhang aufgeht, man kann sie auch nachher nicht wieder so ohne weiteres in den Kasten stecken, wenn man sie nicht mehr gebraucht. Ich möchte Ihnen dieses ein für allemal klarmachen und habe, damit Sie mich recht gut verstehen, ein Gleichnis aus dem Gebiet der Toilette gewählt. Die Kunst ist ein Nessusgewand, unter der schönen, blitzenden Hülle verbrennt man ohne Rettung. Deswegen sind auch ihre Träger nie leichten Herzens; sie haben gerungen, ehe sie es auf sich nahmen, ein selbstloses Dasein zu führen, bewundert vielleicht, aber einsam dabei wie verirrte Kinder, sie alle haben geweint, ehe sie sich darangaben, angestaunt, um früh zu sterben. Was sie aufrechthält, ist einzig und allein ihre edle Begeisterung: die trägt sie auf sturmgeblähten Flügeln hinweg über Zweifel und Leid, über Verzagtheit und schwache Stunden. Und alle wahren Künstler meinen es heilig mit ihrer Kunst. Sie sind meist ernst und schauen wenig unter sich ins Leben; Eifersucht, Neid und ähnliche kleine Erbärmlichkeiten sind ihnen fremd. Dies zu erkennen dürfte für Sie von Vorteil sein, Signora."

Frau Lydias Mund zog sich schlimm zusammen, dennoch legte sie den Kopf auf die Seite, zaghaft und schmeichelnd wie ein gescholtenes Kind.

„Sie zürnen mir, Rossi," sagte sie sanft, „weil Sie wissen, daß ich die kleine Galieri nun einmal nicht leiden kann. Ich kann mich aber nicht bezwingen, ich kann mich nicht anders machen, als ich bin. Glauben Sie etwa," fuhr sie heftiger werdend fort, „daß ich nicht bemerkt habe, wie sehr Sie sich für das Mädchen interessieren, wie sehr Sie sich bemühten, ihr bei der Probe hilfreich zu sein? Ist es wohl erhört, daß der große Rossi sich herbeiläßt, einem solchen Dinge unaufgefordert Ratschläge zu erteilen, daß er es auf die feinsten Nuancen aufmerksam macht? Mich hat es ins Herz getroffen, als Sie ganz laut erklärten, wie sehr es Sie freue, endlich einmal eine Partnerin gefunden zu haben, die keine vokalisierende Puppe sei, sondern die mit der Seele sänge ... und wie leuchteten Ihre Augen, wie sahen Sie, der große Blasierte, auf einmal so jung aus! Ja, die hat es Ihnen gründlich angetan ... ich aber hasse das kokette Milchgesicht und gäbe gern einen Finger darum, wenn sie heut' abend von der Bühne gezischt und für immer in ihr Nichts zurückgeworfen würde! Sehen Sie mich nicht so finster an, ich spreche die Wahrheit: ich verabscheue dieses Mädchen und hasse sie bitter, nicht nur aus gekränktem Künstlerstolz, sondern fast allein deswegen, weil ich Sie, Rossi, so sehr ... weil ich Sie so unendlich verehre ..."

Er verzog wiederum keine Miene, nur seine Hand hob sich zu einer dankenden, müden Bewegung. Sie war jedoch so nachlässig ausgefallen, daß der Sängerin eine Flut von Grimm zum Herzen schoß. Um sich zu rächen, fühlte sie, wie alle wenig zarte Naturen, das Bedürfnis, einen Trumpf auszuspielen, sei er auch noch so verletzend und noch so ungeschickt.

„Spielen Sie keine Komödie!" rief sie höhnisch. „Sie ganz vor allen spekulieren darauf, daß die Kleine durchfällt. Sie hätten dann ja sofort eine prachtvolle Gelegenheit zu Privatnachhilfestunden."

Auf seine Lippen kam ein schlimmes Wort, das er nicht mehr zurückhalten konnte.

„Unsinn," sagte er, „die Trauben hängen für mich zu hoch. Ich habe nur noch bei Frauen zweiter oder dritter Kategorie Glück, wie es scheint auch bei Ihnen, Signora Müller."

Er wandte sich ab, unbekümmert darum, daß Frau

Lydia gelb wurde und eine Ohnmacht vorbereitete. Glücklicherweise wurde die fast unausbleibliche Szene durch das Dazwischenkommen einer dritten Person vereitelt.

„Worüber, wenn man fragen darf, ereifern Sie sich denn so, Frau Müller?" frug gutmütig Pater Heilmann, welcher seine Unterredung beendigt hatte und hinter dem Versatzstücke hervorkam.

„Wir sprachen über Debütantinnen", sagte die Sängerin, indem sie sich gewaltsam bezwang. „Es ist dies ein Thema, für welches Herr Rossi ungewöhnliches Interesse hegt."

Mehrere der Darsteller waren unterdessen herangetreten, es entstand ein Gespräch über Debüts im allgemeinen, welches, da es ein Fachgespräch war, mit großer Lebhaftigkeit geführt wurde. Jeder gedachte dabei des eigenen ersten Auftretens und suchte die komischen Seiten desselben möglichst scherzhaft herauszukehren. Nur Rossi sprach kein Wort, und es kam auch kein Lächeln in das gleichgültige Gesicht mit dem herben Zuge darauf.

„Mein Gott," rief Frau Lydia Müller plötzlich mit ihrer hallenden, etwas hart klingenden Stimme, „da stehen wir, wir arme Sängergesellschaft, und schwatzen von unseren obskuren, für die Mitwelt höchst uninteressanten Debüts, und haben ganz vergessen, unseren großen Kollegen zu fragen, wie das seinige verlief! Er ist ja der einzige unter uns, der die vielerstrebte Höhe glücklich erreicht hat, er ist ja ein Künstler, ein weltberühmter, wirklicher Künstler" — sie weilte auf dem

Worte mit besonderem Nachdruck — „und deswegen muß es für uns alle von Bedeutung sein, zu erfahren, wo und wie er zum erstenmal die Bühne betrat. Nicht wahr, Sie erzählen es uns? Helfen Sie mir doch bitten, meine Herren", setzte sie hinzu, indem sie im Kreise umhersah und halb schmollend, halb eigensinnig mit dem Fuße stampfte.

Der Sänger antwortete ausweichend, mit einem halben Scherze, alle drangen aber so stürmisch in ihn, daß er nachgeben mußte.

„Mein Debüt", begann er endlich, „verlief anders wie die Ihrigen und ließ mir keine besonders heiteren Erinnerungen. Ich war damals noch sehr jung und meinte es ernst mit meiner Kunst, furchtbar ernst, ich hatte mich ihr verschrieben mit Herzblut und Leben. Von meinem ersten Auftreten hing vieles ab, zunächst die Existenz meiner alten Mutter, deren Stütze ich war, ferner das Schicksal meiner ersten und" — er betonte das Wort eigentümlich sicher — „meiner einzigen Liebe. Sie können sich denken, daß ich an jenem Tage keine Landpartie unternahm und auch nicht die ... desinvoltura hatte, meine Rolle schlecht zu studieren. Mein Debüt fand in Bologna statt und ich sang den Figaro im ‚Barbier von Sevilla'."

„Eine Ihrer Glanzrollen", rief der Regisseur, der eben dazugetreten war. „Sie hatten natürlich einen beispiellosen Erfolg?"

„Nein," entgegnete der Sänger einfach, „ich wurde ausgepfiffen."

Eine allgemeine Pause entstand.

„Und jenes junge Mädchen," frug Frau Lydia lauernd, „Ihre erste Liebe, was ist aus ihr geworden?"

„O, ich danke, es geht ihr gut", sagte Rossi. „Sie ist vierzehn Tage darauf mit einem wirklichen Barbier davongelaufen. Aber meine arme Mutter", fügte er leise, wie zu sich selbst hinzu, „ist mir treu geblieben, hat an mich geglaubt und hat mich liebgehabt ihr Leben lang."

Sein Gesicht war mild, seine Stimme ungewöhnlich weich geworden. Draußen entstand plötzlich eine Stille, der Hof war gekommen; dann erhoben sich markig die ersten Klänge der Einleitung. Aus der Garderobe kam Giacinta, sie sah totenblaß aus, aber sehr entschlossen. Als sie an Rossi vorüberging, schlug sie die Augen auf und neigte langsam das Haupt, dann schritt sie quer über die Bühne ihrem Platze zu.

Zwei Stunden später war alles vorbei. Giacinta hatte den ersten Akt und die größte Hälfte des zweiten unter einer Begeisterung des Publikums gesungen, die keine Grenzen kannte, und die, trotz der wundervollen Leistung Rossis, fast einzig der Anfängerin galt. Die große Arie aus E-dur namentlich brachte sie mit so viel Leidenschaft zu Ende, daß sich ein wahrer Sturm erhob; so heftige, reine, seltsam vibrierende Töne hatte man noch nie vernommen. Rossi allein, der an einer Kulisse stand und die Sängerin nicht aus den Augen ließ, machte ein finsteres Gesicht. Der Gang der Handlung rief ihn dann selbst auf die Bühne, und in dem Duett, kaum zehn Minuten später, fiel ihm Giacinta bewußtlos, mit blutigen Lippen in die Arme. Es war ein jäher, unerwarteter Schluß. Das Orchester brach ab, zwischen dem unruhevollen Hause und der leeren Bühne glitt lautlos der Vorhang nieder. Auf einer der obersten Galerien entstand Wortwechsel, ein junger Mann mit verstörten Zügen brach sich durch die festgepreßten Reihen der Sitzenden Bahn. In der Loge des Fürsten kamen und gingen Ordonnanzoffiziere, nach einiger Zeit erschien der Intendant, dann hob sich der Vorhang von neuem und der Regisseur machte unter lautloser Stille die Mitteilung, daß die Oper wegen plötzlicher Erkrankung Fräuleins Galieris nicht zu Ende geführt werden könne. Nach kurzer Pause werde das für morgen angekündigte Ballett in Szene gehen.

Es war eine Neuheit, und das Publikum beruhigte sich bald. Draußen, an einen Laternenpfahl gelehnt, stand Bent. Es war ihm nicht möglich gewesen, Giacinta zu sehen, denn man hatte sie sofort nach ihrer Wohnung gebracht; der Theaterarzt hatte ihm jedoch auf sein Flehen den Bescheid gegeben, daß ihr Zustand nicht gerade besorgniserregend sei. Vermutlich wäre ein Äderchen in der Brust gesprungen, so etwas käme häufig vor. Dann hatte er sich einige scherzhafte, aber nicht sehr diskrete Bemerkungen über das Interesse, welches Bent an Fräulein Galieri zu nehmen schiene, erlaubt und war seiner Wege gegangen. Ein Maschinist frug, ob er angestellt sei oder sonst etwas zu suchen habe, und wies ihm, als er es verneinen mußte, die Tür. So stand er auf der Straße, stumpf gegen alles und wie betäubt. Ein paar Buben, welche vorbeikamen, hielten ihn für betrunken und höhnten ihn, bis ihnen seine Reglosigkeit unheimlich wurde und sie davonliefen. Der Regen rieselte langsam nieder und durchnäßte seinen leichten Rock, er achtete dessen nicht und sah nur starr in die schwarzen Lachen, die an seinen Füßen zusammenliefen. Er wußte nun klar: es ist die Schuld, die sich rächt — auf deinem Wege und dem Giacintas liegt weder Glück noch Stern. „Wenn eine Sühne sein muß, mein Gott," sagte er plötzlich mit fester Stimme, „so erspare sie uns nicht, doch laß uns nicht unter ihr zusammenbrechen. Verlasse du uns nicht, so werden wir nie voneinander lassen."

Er richtete sich auf und ging seiner Wohnung zu. Erst jetzt merkte er, wie sehr ihn der Regen durchnäßt hatte; ein schmerzhaftes Gefühl von Kälte überlief ihn, seine Glieder waren schwer und wie zerschlagen.

Wenn ich jetzt krank würde, dachte er, gerade jetzt, so wäre ja niemand, der über sie wachte ... es darf nicht sein, ich brauche Gesundheit und Kraft, mehr noch als je zuvor.

Drüben war ein großes, hell erleuchtetes Kaffeehaus; er trat ein und verlangte heißen Tee mit etwas Rum. Neben ihm, an zwei zusammengestellten Tischen, saßen Offiziere; sie gehörten dem Reiterregimente des Fürsten an und plauderten lebhaft. Der Lichterglanz und die Wärme taten Bent wohl, ihn überkam ein nicht unangenehmes Gefühl der Mattigkeit, das Klirren der

Gläser und das Gewirr so vieler Stimmen klang zu ihm wie aus weiter Ferne.

„Ich will nur noch ein paar Minuten ruhen," sagte er zu sich selbst; „es ist schön warm hier, und zu Hause finde ich doch kein Feuer mehr."

Plötzlich schlug das Wort „Giacinta" scharf in sein Ohr; es ging unter in einem brausenden Gelächter. Er hob den Kopf und lauschte. Neben ihm, an dem Offizierstische, sprach man von der gewaltsam unterbrochenen Vorstellung, und einer der Herren, ein Rittmeister mit spärlichem Haupthaar und mächtigem blonden Schnurrbarte, schien eben etwas sehr Unterhaltendes gesagt zu haben, denn es dauerte geraume Zeit, bis sich das Lachen gelegt und er sein Glas befriedigt austrinken konnte.

„Ja," sagte ein anderer, „die Sache wird in mehr als einer Beziehung Staub aufgewirbelt haben. Was wird wohl unser guter George dazu sagen? Nun, er hat ja Ableitung für seinen Kummer — paßt einmal auf, die Welt wird der übergeschlagenen Stimme der kleinen Galieri mindestens drei Dutzend Sonette oder ähnliches Zeug zu verdanken haben. Er ist also noch nicht so übel daran, wie der gute Hofrat. Was der für ein Gesicht machen wird, wäre ich in der Tat zu sehen begierig."

„O, der wird gar nicht so unzufrieden sein. Erhält die Kleine, wie ich es beinahe glaube, kein Engagement, so ist sie ja ganz auf ihren Beschützer angewiesen. Dann sollen Sie einmal sehen — bald empfängt Mäcen den süßen Lohn und wird dann den Punkt erreicht haben, um den sich die ganze Geschichte drehte."

„Was diesen höchst interessanten Punkt anbetrifft," nahm der Rittmeister das Wort, „so dürfte er dem Hofrate doch einige leichte Enttäuschungen bereiten. Ich habe gestern so etwas herumgehorcht — bei Frau Lydia unter anderen — und dabei etwas sehr Amüsantes erfahren. Die Kleine ist ein ganz schlaues Pflänzchen: dem guten Hofrate überläßt sie es, ihre Pfade zu ebnen, sie erlaubt ihm selbst, für Toilette und andere Kleinigkeiten zu sorgen — für ihre weiteren Bedürfnisse jedoch hat sie sich einen Liebhaber angeschafft, einen wirklichen Liebhaber. Der Mensch ist eine Art von Student und lebt wahrscheinlich auf ihre Kosten."

„Das ist empörend", sagte ein blutjunger Leutnant, welcher am andern Ende des Tisches saß.

„Empörend? Wo denken Sie hin," lachte der Rittmeister, „im Gegenteil, es ist ganz natürlich und für uns andere sehr angenehm zu wissen! Es geht daraus hervor, daß Fräulein Giacinta ein liebebedürftiges Herz hat ... und wissen Sie nicht, was Valentin im ‚Faust' sagt? Famos das, meine Lieblingsszene:

„Du fingst mit einem heimlich an,
Bald kommen ihrer mehre dran,
Und wenn dich erst ein Dutzend hat,
So ..."

Er konnte nicht ausreden. Ihm gegenüber stand Bent, regungslos, die blutunterlaufenen Augen unheimlich ruhig auf ihn heftend. Seine Erscheinung war so sonderbar, daß am ganzen Tische Totenstille entstand. Er rang mühsam nach Worten; es währte so lange, daß einige der Offiziere sich anblickten und sich zum Fortgehen erhoben.

„Diese verwünschten öffentlichen Kneipen," murmelte einer, „der Mensch ist entschieden geisteskrank."

Bent hörte es nicht, er hatte noch keinen Blick von seinem Gegner verwandt.

„Herr Rittmeister," sagte er mit leiser, heiserer Stimme, „wer eine Frau verleumdet, wes Art sie immer sei, ist ein —"

Er nannte das Wort.

Es war, als habe der Blitz eingeschlagen. Die Herren sprangen auf, der Rittmeister, erdfahl geworden, tastete nach seinem Säbel. Der aber stand, unter Mänteln und Mützen vergraben, in einer Ecke, außerdem hatte einer der älteren Herren sofort den Arm des Beleidigten ergriffen.

„Um Gottes willen," rief er hastig, „nur keinen Eklat. Kommen Sie, meine Herren", sagte er laut zu den übrigen, und zu Bent leise und sehr höflich: „Folgen Sie uns, wenn ich bitten darf; wir werden draußen ungestörter reden können."

Die Offiziere hüllten sich in ihre Mäntel und gingen; die kleine Szene hatte sich so unauffällig abgespielt, daß niemand darauf aufmerksam geworden war. Draußen angekommen, flüsterte der Rittmeister einem der Herren etwas ins Ohr und wandte sich dann zu Bent.

„Sie haben mich beleidigt," sagte er hochfahrend und scharf, indessen seine Hand, die er um den Säbelgriff gelegt, vor Erregung flog, „ich hoffe, daß Sie satisfaktionsfähig sind und für Ihre Worte einstehen werden. Jedenfalls wird Ihnen dieser Herr" — er deutete auf den Leutnant — „nicht eher von den Fersen gehen, bis eine Auseinandersetzung erfolgt ist. Was Sie, meine Herren, anbetrifft," sagte er leise, „so bitte ich vorläufig um Diskretion; die Sache ist eigentlich sehr unangenehm, da es sich, wie es scheint, um einen Studenten oder so etwas ähnliches handelt."

Er grüßte und ging davon, die anderen folgten langsam, unterdrückt plaudernd.

„Es ist natürlich der Mensch, der Liebhaber", scholl es einmal deutlich zurück. Bent hielt wie abwesend die Fäuste geballt, seine Brust hob sich vor schwerer Erregung. Der Leutnant, welcher zurückgeblieben war, berührte leicht seinen Arm.

„Mein Name ist —" hierbei brummte er ein unverständliches Etwas, — „darf ich fragen, mit wem ich den Vorzug habe?"

„Ich heiße Sörensen, bin Studierender an hiesiger Hochschule und werde mich morgen unter die Waffen einer unserer anerkannten Verbindungen stellen."

„Das dürfte nach dem, was vorgefallen, allerdings unerläßlich sein", meinte der Offizier kühl. „Erlauben Sie mir vorläufig eine Frage. Haben Sie irgend ein persönliches Recht, Fräulein Galieri so ... drastisch in Schutz zu nehmen? Sind Sie mit der Dame verwandt?"

„Nein", sagte Bent fest. „Ich bin für sie eingetreten, wie ich's für jede andere Dame täte, die ich öffentlich verleumdet und beleidigt sehe."

Der Offizier verzog höhnisch das Gesicht.

„Hm," meinte er, „so können wir also zu etwas anderem übergehen. Die Bestimmungen, das Duell mit Studenten betreffend, sind, besonders in unserem Regimente, etwas knapp gezogen. Befinden Sie sich in der Lage, mir eine bekannte notable Persönlichkeit zu nennen, bei der ich Erkundigungen über Ihre Verhältnisse, ich will es kurz sagen: über Ihre Satisfaktionsfähigkeit einziehen könnte? Es ist dies kein Mißtrauensvotum," fuhr er fort, als Bent eine heftige Bewegung machte, „es ist eine reine Formalität und würde den Gang der Angelegenheit bedeutend beschleunigen."

„Ich kenne fast niemand," sagte Bent rauh, „wenden Sie sich jedoch an den Hofrat — erst kürzlich hat er geruht, mich seiner vollen Protektion zu versichern."

„An wen?" frug der Offizier in gedehntem Tone. Er glaubte nicht richtig gehört zu haben.

„An den Herrn Hofrat, der ebenfalls die Ehre hatte, Gegenstand Ihres vorherigen Gesprächsthemas zu sein."

„So? An den Hofrat? Sonderbar ... jedenfalls würde somit jeder Zweifel, der über Ihre Person noch walten könnte, beseitigt sein. Ich bitte Sie also, mir bis morgen früh elf Uhr Ihre Sekundanten senden zu wollen. Dabei erlaube ich mir, Ihnen zu bemerken, daß nach unseren ehrengerichtlichen Bestimmungen die Sekundanten graduierte oder chargierte Persönlichkeiten von unbestreitbarer Satisfaktionsfähigkeit sein müssen. Es wird Ihnen gewiß nicht schwer fallen, jemanden zu finden, der Ihnen diesen Dienst erweisen könnte."

„Ich hatte bereits die Ehre, Ihnen zu sagen,“ entgegnete Bent, „daß ich in hiesiger Stadt sehr wenig gute Bekannte zähle, auf die ich bauen könnte. Ich habe jedoch einen Freund, der sich meiner Angelegenheit annehmen und Ihren Bestimmungen hoffentlich genügen wird. Sein Name ist von Versen.“

Der Offizier trat einen Schritt zurück, indem er einen Ausruf des Erstaunens nicht unterdrücken konnte.

„Versen? George von Versen? Der Sohn des verstorbenen Ministers? Aber der ist ja Reserveoffizier in unserem Regiment ...“

„Mag sein,“ erwiderte Bent, „ich wußte es nicht. Jedenfalls werde ich mich, wenn Sie es erlauben, Herr Leutnant, sofort zu ihm begeben.“

Er grüßte und ging davon. Der Offizier sah ihm nach und blieb noch eine gute Weile kopfschüttelnd stehen. Ihn erfüllte ein leitender Gedanke, nämlich der, daß der Herr Rittmeister möglicherweise an eine ganz unrechte Haustür geraten sein könne. —

Zehn Minuten später klingelte Bent an dem Versenschen Hause. Er war rasch gegangen, in seinem Ohr lag noch das wüste Gelächter, mit welchem die Offiziere Giacintas Namen begraben hatten. Ein weißköpfiger Diener öffnete und führte ihn durch einen Garten voll hoher Taxushecken, aus deren Dunkel zuweilen die Schultern einer Marmorstatue hervorleuchteten, nach einem kleinen zweistöckigen Nebengebäude.

„Der junge Herr ist bei der gnädigen Frau Mutter,“ sagte er, „ich werde Sie sogleich melden.“

Dann öffnete er eine Tür und zog sich geräuschlos, mit stummer Verbeugung zurück.

Bent durchflog das Zimmer, in welchem er sich befand, trotz seiner Erregung, mit erstaunten, fast scheuen Blicken. Versen mußte ja ganz ungeheuer reich sein; daran hatte er nie gedacht und es eigentlich auch nicht für möglich gehalten, daß ein junger Mann, welcher studierte, überhaupt reich sein könne. Im Kamine brannte, der feuchten Witterung halber, ein leichtes Feuer. Er trat schüchtern näher, wärmte sich und betrachtete neugierig die vielen fremdartigen Gegenstände, den weichen Teppich, die niedrigen, behaglichen Sessel, den breiten Schreibtisch von Eichenholz, mit Büchern und Schriften bedeckt, den Kopf des Elchhirschs da oben mit den dunklen, riesigen Schaufeln, die Waffen an der Wand, in denen sich das flackernde Feuer zuweilen rötlich spiegelte. Dann wehte ihn ein feiner Duft an; in einer Ecke stand ein Blumentisch, drauf eine Fülle blaßblauer Veilchen blühte. Er beugte sich nieder, so daß die kühlen Blumenkelche seine Stirn streiften; ihr Hauch gemahnte ihn an den Duft von Giacintas weichem Haar. Er erhob sich und griff mit der Hand an die Stirne, dann hörte er, wie der Vorhang zurückgeschlagen wurde und George ins Zimmer trat.

George ging hastig auf ihn zu und grüßte ihn.

„Es freut mich, daß ich dich sehe, Bent," sagte er erregt und abgebrochen, „gerade heute bist du mir doppelt willkommen. Ich bin in keiner guten Stimmung, denn es ist etwas geschehen, was mich sehr schmerzlich ergriffen hat. Setze dich", fügte er hinzu, indem er die Lampe hinaufschraubte, so daß ein mildes, volles Licht durchs Zimmer flog. „Weißt du auch, daß es für einen Freund nicht hübsch ist, volle acht Tage nichts von sich hören zu lassen? Himmel, Bent, wie siehst du aus!" rief er, indem er sich jäh erhob. „Was ist mit dir geschehen? Bist du krank?"

„Höre", sagte Bent mit unsicherer Stimme. „Du hast mir in einem Augenblicke der Erregung Freundschaft geschworen, aber um mich taumelt alles, stürzt alles. George, ich komme zu dir hilfesuchend, ein unglücklicher, zerschlagener Mensch; bist du wirklich mein Freund und willst du mir helfen?"

„Ich bin es, Bent, auf Leben und Tod. Alles, was mein ist, ist dein. Sage einfach, was dir fehlt, und zweifle nicht an mir."

„Ich frug dich auch nur deshalb noch einmal," sagte Bent mit einem unbeschreiblich wehmütigen Lächeln, „weil ich erst jetzt gesehen habe, daß du sehr reich bist. Nun ist aber alles gut. Höre mich an; ich komme aus dem Theater, wo heute eine junge Sängerin, Fräulein Galieri, zum erstenmal aufgetreten ist. Sie ist krank geworden und wird wahrscheinlich nicht wieder engagiert werden ..."

Er schwieg einen Augenblick, um Mut zu gewinnen, Versens Augen lagen auf ihm mit dem Ausdrucke des höchsten Erstaunens.

„Ich ging nachher in ein Kaffeehaus, um etwas Heißes zu trinken, denn ich fühlte mich erschöpft. Neben mir an einem Tische saßen Offiziere; sie sprachen über die verunglückte Vorstellung und über Fräulein Galieri, und einer von ihnen, ein Rittmeister, sagte ..." hier brach seine Stimme vor Scham und Schmerz, „daß sie vom Hofrat Geld annähme und einen heimlichen Liebhaber besäße, der auf ihre Kosten lebe ..."

Versen sprang auf, eine dunkle, fliegende Röte schoß über sein Gesicht, indes es in seinen Augen aufblitzte wie von tödlichem Grimm.

„O," sagte er endlich mit bebender, tiefer Stimme, „ich habe nun einmal kein Glück im Leben. O Gott, wäre ich statt deiner dagewesen und hätte ich ..."

„Laß mich ausreden, George. Ich sagte dem Rittmeister, daß er ein Verleumder sei. Die Herren entfernten sich sofort und ich hatte mit einem derselben eine Auseinandersetzung, die Genugtuung betreffend, die ich werde geben müssen. Ich nannte deinen Namen, was den Herrn sehr zu überraschen schien — er sagte, du seiest Reserveoffizier in seinem Regimente — und nun wollte ich dich bitten, George, mir in der Sache beizustehen. Ich habe ja keinen Freund außer dir und werde mich auch bemühen, dir in Zukunft nie wieder Umständlichkeiten zu verursachen."

Er schwieg und hob den Blick schüchtern zu Versen empor. Der stand regungslos am Kamin; es gehörte Bents ganze Erregung dazu, um ihn die furchtbare Veränderung, die in den Zügen des Freundes geschehen war, übersehen zu lassen. Es ward eine Pause, endlich strich Versen wie geistesabwesend mit der Hand über die Stirn.

„Möchtest du mir sagen," frug er mühsam, „aus welchem Grunde du dich in die Unterhaltung der Offiziere gemischt hast? Leitete dich nur der ehrenwerte Trieb, einer angegriffenen wehrlosen Frau beizustehen, oder hattest du" — er würgte die Worte tonlos heraus — „ein Anrecht, für Fräulein Galieri einzutreten?"

„Dieselbe Frage," sagte Bent, „stellte der Offizier, mit welchem ich verhandelte. Ich habe ihm die Wahrheit nicht gesagt, es ist schlimm genug, daß ich einen Ehrenmann habe belügen müssen. Es konnte aber nicht anders sein, George", er stockte und ballte die Fäuste so fest, daß sich die Nägel ins Fleisch gruben, dann warf er sich wild an Versens Brust. Die Erregung, die ihn so lange künstlich aufrechterhalten hatte, brach zusammen, er schluchzte ungestüm wie ein Kind. „George," sagte er endlich, „ich liebe Giacinta und sie ist mein vor Gott."

Über Versens Antlitz flog eine Blässe, so jäh und tief, als sei der letzte Blutstropfen daraus gewichen; als Bent jedoch das Haupt erhob, sah er nur ein stilles Gesicht, das ernst und vornehm auf ihn niederblickte.

„Willst du mir beistehen, George?" frug er mit klarer Stimme.

Sein Geständnis hatte ihn erleichtert, eine sichere, fast freudige Ruhe war über ihn gekommen.

„Gewiß," antwortete Versen, „sei über den Gang der Sache ganz unbesorgt. Was den Hofrat anbetrifft, so bin ich in der Lage, dir einige Aufklärungen geben zu können. Er ist ein Ehrenmann. Er hat alles Erdenkliche getan, um Fräulein Galieri den Weg zu ebnen und ihr ein Auftreten zu ermöglichen. Ich glaube, er tat es mit blutendem Herzen, denn er mußte sich, wie übrigens jeder denkende Mensch, sagen, daß dieses vom Feuer der Kunst verzehrte Kind viel zu zart, viel zu knospenhaft für den Frondienst der Bühne sei. Dasselbe sagt auch jeder, der sie nur einmal gesehen hatte, und ich glaube, sie selbst mochte es wohl am besten wissen von allen."

„Hast du Giacinta gekannt?" frug Bent seinerseits mit Erstaunen.

„Ja," sagte Versen, indem er einen unglücklichen Versuch machte, zu lächeln, „aber beruhige dich, ich habe sie nur ein paarmal in Gesellschaften, beim Hofrat oder bei meiner Mutter, gesehen. Nun aber rate ich dir, dich schlafen zu legen; du bist angegriffen, und die Uhr geht auf Mitternacht. Morgen werde ich bei dir sein, um deine Sache ganz geschäftsmäßig in Ordnung zu bringen. Sei guten Mutes und quäle dich nicht; blicke auch nicht so trüb in die Zukunft: ich habe geschworen, dein Freund zu sein, und werde mein Wort halten um jeden Preis, es möge geschehen, was da wolle. Schlimmeres kann überhaupt nicht kommen", sprach er bitter und unhörbar zu sich selbst.

Bent reichte ihm überwallend beide Hände, George machte eine gewaltsame Anstrengung und ergriff sie. Als die Tür zufiel, schlug er die Hände vors Gesicht und ließ sich in einen Sessel fallen. So blieb er lange, dann ging er plötzlich an den Schreibtisch und nahm ein flaches Kästchen von dunkelrotem Samt heraus. Darin lag ein Bild von Giacinta, er hatte es selbst gezeichnet, meisterhaft, und doch nur aus der Erinnerung. Es war ein süßes Bild, das feine Köpfchen schien ihn wehmütig anzublicken. Er beugte sich eine Weile darüber und preßte es an die Augen, dann warf er es rasch ins lodernde Kaminfeuer.

„Gute Ruh'," sagte er, „du reiner, kurzer Traum. Du meine erste und letzte Liebe — leb wohl."

* *
*

Bent konnte Giacinta am anderen Tage nicht sehen, doch sandte sie ihm ein Briefchen mit zwei mühsam gekritzelten Zeilen: es ginge ihr besser, er möge sich nicht ängstigen. Am nächsten Morgen, bei Tagesanbruch, fuhr er mit Versen ins Land hinaus. Der Kutscher hing fröstelnd auf seinem Sitze, fest in eine alte Pferdedecke gewickelt, zuweilen ließ er müde und gelangweilt einen Peitschenhieb auf die mageren Mähren fallen.

Es war ein häßlicher Morgen; über endlosen, regennassen Feldern hoben sich blaugrau die Umrisse eines Waldes.

„Da ist's," sagte Versen lakonisch; „ich wollte, ich wäre an deiner Stelle, Bent."

Der Wagen hielt, vier oder fünf Herren in Uniform schritten, gleichgültig plaudernd, durchs nasse Gras, ein anderer stand abseits und schien mit einem Kasten beschäftigt, den er auf einen flachen, an der Wurzel geschlagenen Stamm gestellt hatte.

„Bleib hier," sagte Versen beim Aussteigen, „ich muß mit den Herren reden. So will es einmal die Komödie."

Er nahm den Säbel auf, denn auch er war in voller Uniform, und näherte sich der Gruppe. Man schien eifrig zu sprechen, man verneigte sich gegenseitig und trennte sich. Einer riß Baumzweige ab und steckte sie in den Boden, der Rittmeister nahm seine Zigarre aus dem Munde und klemmte sie zwischen die Zweige einer kleinen silberweißen Buche, die neben ihm stand.

„Hierher, Bent, wenn ich bitten darf", sagte Versen mit kalter, befehlender Stimme.

Ein anderer Herr trat heran und reichte Bent eine halb gespannte Pistole.

„Nach dem Kommando Feuer", sagte er, „zähle ich bis drei, Sie haben in dieser Zeit zu schießen, weder vorher noch nachher. Haben Sie mich verstanden?"

Bent bejahte.

Versen trat zu ihm und sagte:

„Sei ruhig und spanne wenigstens den Hahn deiner Pistole. So!" Und bei sich selbst sprach er: Adieu, Bent.

Er trat zur Seite.

„Sind die Herren fertig? Feuer! Eins — zwei —"

Bent hatte den Rittmeister gegenüber, er suchte instinktmäßig dessen Brust und quälte sich an dem Abzuge der Waffe ab.

Er fühlte einen Schlag und lag lang im Grase, bei voller Besinnung. Er sah ein Rauchwölkchen, das sich über die feuchte Schonung hob, er sah Versen, der auf ihn zustürzte und den Arm um seinen Nacken legte. Auf der anderen Seite kniete bereits der Arzt, durchdringenden Blickes vorgebeugt. Er hob forschend Bents Augenlider, dann riß er die Kleider auf und tastete schnell an der Brust herum.

„Heben Sie den Arm,“ befahl er, „so — nun atmen Sie einmal tief, recht tief.“ Er legte sein Ohr an Bents Brust und erhob sich. „Ich hoffe nicht,“ sagte er zu den übrigen, „daß die Lunge verletzt ist. Die Kugel sitzt zwischen Schlüsselbein und erster Rippe; in sechs Wochen kann er aus der gröbsten Gefahr sein.“

Die Sekundanten verließen ihre Plätze; der Rittmeister griff sofort nach seiner Zigarre, welche noch brannte, und steckte sie in den Mund.

„Ich werde zunächst auf Urlaub gehen,“ sagte er mit leichter Verbeugung, „besten Dank also, meine Herren; seien Sie so gut, lieber Doktor, mir möglichst oft Nachricht über das Befinden des Herrn Sörensen zukommen zu lassen.“

Man trennte sich. Versen führte, mit Hilfe des Doktors, Bent zum Wagen, bettete ihn sorglich in die Kissen und befahl dem Kutscher, langsam nach der Stadt zu fahren. Ernst und schweigend blickte er ins blasse Gesicht des Freundes, der zuweilen die Augen aufschlug und ihm matt zulächelte. Am Tore ließ der Doktor halten und kletterte aus dem Wagen.

„Ich habe heute Lazarettinspektion,“ sagte er, „und daher keine Minute zu verlieren, jedenfalls werde ich aber sofort einen meiner Kollegen vom Zivil senden. Auch wäre es besser, wenn Sie, Herr von Versen, mit mir ausstiegen und Ihren Freund, um Aufsehen zu vermeiden, allein nach Hause fahren ließen. Er kann sehr gut ohne Hilfe die Treppe hinauf und ins Bett kommen. Fühlen Sie sich dazu nicht stark genug?" frug er, indem er sich an Bent wandte.

„Gewiß," versetzte dieser hastig, „Sie kommen meinem Wunsche nur zuvor. Bitte, George, laß mich," fügte er hinzu, als Versen eine Einwendung machte; „du kannst mich ja in ein paar Stunden besuchen. Ich möchte gerne so unbemerkt wie möglich mein Zimmer erreichen."

Aus seinem Wesen sprach eine krankhafte Sucht, allein zu sein, seine Augen blitzten, seine Wangen waren leicht gerötet. Versen sah ihn prüfend an, ehe er den Wagenschlag freigab.

„Er hat jetzt schon Wundfieber", sagte er zu dem kleinen Doktor, der bereits ein paar Schritte vorausgekeucht war.

„Freilich, freilich, Herr Baron," antwortete dieser, „wenn Sie gegen Abend zu ihm kommen, kennt er Sie nicht mehr."

Sie gingen schweigend weiter.

„Hören Sie, lieber Doktor," sagte Versen, plötzlich stehen bleibend, „keine Komödie zwischen uns. Wird er sterben oder nicht?"

„Sterben? Hm — Sie haben eine Art zu interpellieren, die ziemlich direkt ist. Sterben! Wer kann das sagen? Die Wunde ist an und für sich nicht tödlich, aber der junge Mann hat ein entschieden nervöses Temperament, was für einen Heilprozeß immerhin ungünstig ist. Er sah mir außerdem moralisch affiziert und überreizt aus ... jedenfalls würde dem Rittmeister die gleiche Verwundung weniger geschadet haben ... der hat eine wahre Riesennatur, ein prachtvoll phlegmatisches, unerschütterliches Temperament. Der Mann wird älter werden als ich und Ihr Freund, so viel steht fest."

„Sie irren sich, lieber Doktor," sagte Versen; „diesmal stellten Sie eine gründlich falsche Diagnose. Der Rittmeister ist ebenso krank wie Bent Sörensen — stirbt mein Freund, so überlebt er ihn höchstens um vierundzwanzig Stunden."

„Ich verstehe Sie nicht, verehrter Herr, Sie sprechen in Rätseln. Aber was ist Ihnen? Sie sehen ganz unheimlich aus ..."

„Ich hätte Sie für hellhöriger gehalten, bester Doktor", sagte Versen, indem sein schönes Gesicht sich entstellte. „Ich bin ein alter Jäger und kenne den Grabschuß — wenn Bent Sörensen stirbt, so stirbt auch der Herr Rittmeister. Und nun wünsche ich Ihnen einen vergnügten Tag, lieber Doktor."

Bent hatte unterdessen den Wagen verlassen und stieg, die Zähne zusammenbeißend, die Stirn von Schweiß bedeckt die steile Treppe hinauf. Glücklicherweise begegnete ihm niemand, die Kinder waren in der Schule, die Dienstmädchen noch auf dem Markt. Selbst die Tür zu Frau Bitterlichs Flur stand offen; die grollende Dame hörte wohl den Schritt ihres Mieters, wandte aber schon längst nicht mehr den Kopf nach ihm um. Als Bent sein Zimmer glücklich erreicht hatte, ließ er sich schwer auf einen Stuhl fallen; ein quälender Gedanke stieg in ihm auf. Die Osterferien waren vor der Tür, er hätte sie, fester Verabredung gemäß, bei den Eltern verleben sollen; der alte Pastor gedachte wohl, dem Sohne nach zweijähriger Abwesenheit wieder einmal ins Herz zu sehen. Nun aber — die zerschossene Schulter, die sechs Wochen Krankenlager — was sollte daraus werden? Die Eltern durften ja um keinen Preis wissen, daß er einen Zweikampf bestanden, die Mutter würde sich zu Tode grämen und der Vater die Hand von dem abziehen, der in mörderischer Absicht die Waffe gegen einen Mitmenschen erhoben hatte. Was also beginnen, welches Mittel anwenden, um die Heimreise zu hintertreiben?

Bent sann ängstlich nach, er fühlte unklar, daß die Minuten, die ihm übrigblieben, gezählt seien. Er schleppte sich endlich an den Tisch, nahm ein Blatt Papier und schrieb:

„Geliebte Eltern!

Zu meinem Bedauern kann ich nicht zu Euch kommen, wie ich's so gerne gewollt. Ein russischer Fürst will mich für die Dauer der Ferien nach Italien mitnehmen, ich kann es durchaus nicht ablehnen, weil es für meine Zukunft von hoher Bedeutung sein kann ..."

Der arme Junge! Während er diesen Unsinn niederschrieb, flog seine Hand so, daß die Zeilen schief über dem Blatte zusammenliefen. Er merkte es nicht und siegelte mit großer Anstrengung, dann wurde es ihm schwarz vor Augen und er fiel lang über das Bett hin. Der Verband hatte sich gelöst, ein schmaler Blutstreifen sickerte über Frau Bitterlichs schöne weiße Kissen und tröpfelte langsam auf die wohlgescheuerte Diele. Es wurde Abend. —

Bent lag ohne Besinnung, er erwachte auch nicht, als man die Kugel und später Splitter des zerschossenen Schlüsselbeins entfernte. Die schwere, lähmende Nacht, welche auf ihm lag, raubte jede Empfindung und machte ihn für äußere Eindrücke gefühllos. Zuweilen war es ihm, als kreise sein Haupt; ein Ton brauste darin gleich dem Singen eines Glases, über dessen Rand man streicht. Dann legte sich eine kühle, schmale Hand auf seine Stirn, in die Schwüle, die ihn umfing, wehte es hinein wie Veilchenduft, und er atmete tief auf in unbewußter Erleichterung. So rannen langsam die Tage, plötzlich schien es dem Kranken, als wiche ein Schleier von seinen Augen, er empfand eine unsägliche Beklemmung, sein ganzes Wesen bäumte sich auf und rang nach Bewußtsein. Eine donnernde Stimme, die er gut, nur zu gut kannte, war in sein Ohr gefallen, die Worte hatten in sein fieberndes Hirn geschlagen wie schwere eiserne Nägel.

„Der Platz an diesem Lager ist mein! Ich allein werde meinen Sohn zu heilen wissen ..."

Er schlug mit übermenschlicher Anstrengung die Augen auf und richtete sich empor, allein seine linke Seite war gelähmt, mit einem Ächzen des Schmerzes sank er zurück. Die Fenster waren verhängt, aus dem halbdunklen Zimmer glitt eine Gestalt, das Haupt gesenkt, ein Schluchzen auf den Lippen. Am Bette stand ein riesenhafter Greis, den Arm erhoben, mit fürchterlichem Gesicht nach der Türe deutend.

Und nun begann das Werk des orthodoxen lutherischen

Priesters. Wohl eine Stunde lang währte die donnernde Rede; mit Elternfluch, Verdammnis und allen Schrecknissen der Bibel wurde auf den Bewußtlosen, der sich stöhnend in den Kissen wand, eingewirkt. Zuletzt mußte er ein Schreiben unterzeichnen, welches der Pastor verfaßt. Die knochigen Finger des Greises zwängten der Hand des Sohnes die Feder ein und führten sie über das Papier, dann kam der Arzt und erlöste den Kranken. Während der in schwülem, unruhigem Halbschlummer lag, saß der Pastor am Tische und schrieb nach Hause. Es war ein langer Brief, eine Stelle darin lautete:

„Dem Herrn Herrn sei Preis! Die Bathseba ward vertrieben — wir haben unsern Sohn wieder."

* * *

Er hatte sich fast geirrt, der starre lutherische Priester! Ein furchtbares Nervenfieber brachte Bent an den Rand des Grabes, es währte sehr lange, ehe es besser mit ihm wurde. Und unterdessen vollzog sich auch das Schicksal Giacintas, langsam, unerbittlich, trotz schwerer Kämpfe, die ihre Seele müde machten für immer. Die Welt nannte dieses Schicksal ein glückliches. Es durften die beiden nicht sterben, weil sie sich tief geliebt — sie sollten leben, um voneinander zu lassen. An einem weichen, grauen Märztage hielten eine Reihe glänzender Equipagen am Portale der Domkirche; aus der ersten stieg der Hofrat, Giacinta am Arm. Ihnen folgte Madame Galieri, sie trug ein gelbseidenes Kleid gewagtesten Schnittes und schwamm in Seligkeit; sie hing am

Arme eines Herrn, dessen Brust mit Sternen bedeckt war, und der sich beeilte, mit seiner Bürde die Stufen hinaufzukommen. Die Kirche war voller Menschen, durch die gemalten Fenster brach trüb der Schein des Regentags. Der Hochaltar strahlte von Kerzen, über ihm lag eine feine, leise verschwebende Weihrauchwolke; die Seitenschiffe waren ganz dunkel, die mächtigen Pfeiler düsterbunt beleuchtet. Es erwachte die Orgel, präludierend mit einer einfachen Weise, dann voller werdend, brausend in tiefen, gewaltigen Akkorden, zum Lichte ringend wie Auferstehungsklang, ausströmend in breiter, festlicher Lösung. Es ward tiefes Schweigen, in die Stille fielen langsam die Worte des Priesters, draußen rauschte der Regen und der Tauwind brauste um die Johannistürme ... dann gingen tieftönig die Glocken, das Volk drängte nach den Portalen, und über die Massen hinweg brandeten die letzten Töne des Gloria. Aus dem dunklen Seitenschiffe traten zwei Menschen und schritten dem Altar zu. Der eine war ein Greis mit hartem, vergrämtem Gesichte, er stützte sorgsam seinen krankhaft zusammengefallenen Sohn. Vor dem Altar blieb der Alte stehen, er mochte nicht herantreten, sondern betrachtete finster die goldenen Meßgeräte; der Kranke dagegen schritt durch das niedrige Gitter und über den Teppich, der die Stufen deckte. Dort lag ein seidenes Kissen, auf welchem eine Minute vorher Giacinta gekniet, daneben ein paar welke Veilchen, dem Hochzeitsstrauße entfallen, auch ein schmaler Streifen, achtlos vom Brautschleier gerissen. Er nahm das alles auf und barg es an seiner Brust, dann stürzte er über dem Kissen zusammen, legte die Stirn in die Hände und weinte.

* * *

Bent hat Giacinta nie wiedergesehen. Er hat ein Jahr später sein Examen mit knapper Not bestanden und darauf die ersehnte Stelle erhalten.

Seine Familie ist nun versorgt, der Pfarrer hat zuweilen einen Braten auf dem Tisch und kann für die jüngsten Kinder das Schulgeld aufbringen. Bent hat sich im Innersten von seiner Fachwissenschaft abgewandt, er ist seltsamerweise Dichter geworden. Eine Handvoll Lieder, die er an Giacinta gerichtet, erregte Staunen und brachte ihm fast den Ruhm; es war sein erstes und bestes Werk. Was er später geschrieben, ist schroff oder unklar; man ahnt wohl das Vorhandensein einer Kraft, fühlt aber sofort, daß diese Kraft früh und im Kerne gebrochen ward. Er wird es nie zu etwas bringen; man liest ihn sogar in seinem Vaterlande, wo man doch junge Talente gern beschützt, nur wenig. Giacinta ist eine schöne stille Frau und dem alternden Hofrat eine treue Pflegerin geworden. Sie hat nie wieder gesungen und liest keine Gedichte mehr, selbst nicht diejenigen Bents. Was George von Versen anbetrifft, so ist er auf Reisen gegangen, von denen man nur selten zurückkehrt. Sie alle sind untergegangen in den Tauwassern.

www.ingramcontent.com/pod-product-compliance
Lightning Source LLC
La Vergne TN
LVHW092105300926
849161LV00002B/47
* 9 7 8 3 1 1 2 6 3 5 5 7 5 *